EFFECTIVE INTERVIEWING FOR EMPLOYMENT SELECTION

Clive T. Goodworth

BUSINESS BOOKS
London Melbourne Sydney Auckland Johannesburg

Business Books Ltd
An imprint of the Hutchinson Publishing Group
17 Conway Street , London W1P 6JD

Hutchinson Group (Australia) Pty Ltd
30-32 Cremorne Street, Richmond South, Victoria 3121
PO Box 151, Broadway, New South Wales 2007

Hutchinson Group (NZ) Ltd
32-34 View Road, PO Box 40-086, Glenfield, Auckland 10

Hutchinson Group (SA) (Pty) Ltd
PO Box 337, Bergvlei 2012, South Africa

First published 1979
Second impression with revisions 1983

Set in IBM Press Roman

Printed in Great Britain by the Anchor Press Ltd
and bound by Wm Brendon & Son Ltd
both of Tiptree, Essex

British Library Cataloguing In Publication Data
Goodworth, Clive T.
    Effective interviewing for employment selection.
    1. Employment interviewing
    I. Title
    658.3'1124   HF5549.5.16

ISBN 0 09 150330 2 (Cased)
     0 09 150331 0 (Paperback)

To all interviewers 'Who know a good chap when they see one' —

To all candidates who suffer under them
— *this book*

CONTENTS

ILLUSTRATIONS

SELF-TUTORIALS

PREFACE

Hope springs eternal in them thar selection hills . . . There is growing evidence that many companies and individual managers are beginning to display a healthy interest in the art of conducting effective employment interviews. More power to your elbow, Mr Executive-in-the-Hot-Seat, and if this book helps you to pick the wheat from the candidate chaff — why, all well and good!

My thanks to those who commented kindly on the First Impression and for the many interesting letters I have received.

CLIVE GOODWORTH
November 1981

Her father lov'd me; oft invited me;
Still question'd me the story of my life,
From year to year, the battles, sieges, fortunes
That I have pass'd.
I ran it through, even from my boyish days
To the very moment that he bade me tell it . . .

Shakespeare, 'Othello'

1

SO WE INTERVIEW — BUT WHAT ARE WE LOOKING FOR?

The process of selecting employees by interview is as old as employment itself. Faced with the task of picking the best from a band of strangers, the employer can use records and recommendations from other people in an attempt to infer future behaviour from this secondhand knowledge of the candidates' past — but the face-to-face interview will cement his decision. The fact is that the interview has been the principal tool of selection for so long that it is often continued even though there may be no clearly defined objective indicating what the process is to accomplish. It is largely due to this unquestioning faith in interviewing as a tradition — as part of the very fabric of business itself — that few employers give any consideration to the vital necessity for training in the technique. Despite a volume of evidence over many years that interview judgements are often inadequate, biased and always highly subjective, there has been little or nothing in the way of tangible pressure on employers to justify a change in this happily complacent attitude. But that was yesterday.

The acceptance of the successful candidate, the marriage ceremony of man and job, is now permeated with the sinister overtones of a drastic and often expensive divorce procedure. *'Each employee shall have the right not to be unfairly dismissed by his employer, and the remedy of an employee so dismissed. . . . . .shall be by way of complaint to an industrial tribunal.'* The chilling provisions of Great Britain's employment law — to name but one thorn in the unsuspecting flesh of the complacent

1

employer – strike directly at the heart of his selection procedures. The message is dire and simple; bad selection can cost a great deal of money. It behoves the employer, more than ever before, to look to his interviewing laurels.

A face-to-face interview is necessary and well justified in terms of the human relations value involved; *its purpose is to carry out a comprehensive and accurate background investigation – to seek out and verify the facts of past achievement and failure.* The name of the interviewing game is *perception* and *prediction.* The technique must enable the interviewer, having perceived the facts, to form a valid and reliable prediction of the candidate's future performance in a given role in comparison with the predictions made for other candidates. This is no mean task. The crux of such personal, face-to-face assessment is that information about the candidate filters through the highly subjective screen of the interviewer's own views, needs and prejudices. In short, the interview is not an *objective* tool of selection.

A fully objective selection process is one in which every assessor inspecting a certain performance arrives at precisely the same report. To achieve this measure of objectivity, the same degree of attention must be paid to exactly the same aspects of the performance. The human brain – and thank God for it – is utterly incapable of performing in this manner. That which is 'good' in the eyes of one man is merely 'average' in the eyes of another. John's view of the essential ingredients of, say, 'leadership' varies with that held by Jack. We are all different and, when it comes to weighing up people and pronouncing on their qualities, our individual scales have infinite variance. There is really only one way in which the interviewer may partly overcome the barrier of his innate subjectivity, and that is to recognise the characteristics of his own views and prejudices. Very fortunately, there are some characteristics – or, to be precise, failings – which are common to a great number of interviewers.

The Halo Error   An interviewer tends to judge a candidate in terms of a general attitude towards the subject's personality as a whole. Thus, it may happen that the average healthy male – when faced with a particularly delectable young miss who aspires to be his secretary – will tend to over-rate her typing ability. Those gorgeous legs have had their halo effect. . . . Similarly, the interviewer who is an ardent golfer, having discovered that a candidate shares his love for the game, may tend to over-rate the applicant in terms of highly different qualities. It must always be remembered that an individual can be rich in one quality and lacking in another – and almost certainly is.

2

The Logical Error   This is a dangerous pitfall for the inexperienced interviewer. He is very often inclined to arrive at similar assessments in respect of qualities that *seem* logically related. The candidate who gives every appearance of being a quick thinker may *not* possess a high degree of intelligence. The poor applicant who possesses a 'foxy' countenance, with deep-set and 'mean-looking' eyes, may *not* be a devious scoundrel.

The Error of Leniency   Again, there is a tendency for inexperienced interviewers to exercise undue leniency with candidates. When placed on the hot-seat and required to justify an over-lenient assessment, such timid souls usually protest that they cannot bring themselves to be 'too hard' on a candidate. The fact that their error may well land an applicant in the unhappy situation of trying to cope with a job that is totally unsuitable never seems to occur to these interviewers.

The Mirror-image Error   Who will be man enough to admit to this failing? The creed is simple: 'I know I am good — therefore, to be good, he must be like me'. Beware of the interviewer, Mr Boss, who tells you that he knows exactly what he seeking in a candidate — he is probably in the grip of mirror-image fever. The honest interviewer who recognises this failing in himself is well on the way to success.

The Contrast Error   The sinister opposite to the mirror-image syndrome. Too many interviewers tend to assess others in the opposite direction to themselves in given qualities. The reason is self-preservation, pure and simple — it happens and it must not.

Having discovered, albeit painfully, that it is necessary for an interviewer to examine the peculiar characteristics of his own views and prejudices — what then? The next task is to evaluate the nature and potential value of the information to be sought during the interview process. Luckily, research has provided some important milestones on this particular road to effective selection.

Skill   The quality of skill, which involves the ability to coordinate mind and body in the efficient performance of relatively complicated operations, is recognised as the most universally considered quality. Some jobs require varying degrees of many types of skill, e.g. mental, reading and reasoning, and certain positions require specific combinations. Other jobs, such as tool and die making, require certain levels of specific skills. The identification of candidates' skills is an essential pre-requisite to any selection process.

3

Experience   The value of experience has had wide acceptance in the selection world. Most recruitment advertisements specify some form of experience as a required qualification for the job — which poses the question: where *do* 'starters' find work?

Age   Experience may be closely related to age and, conversely, age may be regarded as a very approximate measure of a candidate's experience. The somewhat hackneyed story of the job advertisement which, having quoted an upper age limit of 25, then requires 10 years' experience, has some foundation in fact. Many authorities have questioned the recent emphasis by employers on recruiting youth to the helm. There is growing evidence that the practice of lightly discarding experience and wisdom in preference for youth is a some-what risky business. Employers — tread warily.

Sex   The question of sex and employment is now hopelessly enveloped in the vast and often pure cloud-cuckoo ramifications of *The Sex Discrimination Act, 1975* — but this must not deter an employer from closely examining the requirements of the job concerned. As is well known, the legislation permits exceptions to be made in cases where a person's sex can be shown to be a 'genuine occupational qualification' and — hilarity apart — the possibility of such a qualification must be fully exploited.

Education and Training   These qualifications obviously provide corroborative evidence of the abilities of the individual and, in many cases, levels of education and training are specified for the jobs concerned. It should be noted that many 'qualifications' gained in adult life, e.g. membership of certain societies and institutes, do not entail study or qualifying examinations — or, for that matter, entry on the basis of experience. A further point to remember is that the educational system in the United Kingdom has been subjected to considerable change in recent years — older interviewers, do your homework.

Physical Qualities   Certain job specifications may require specific physical qualities, such as strength, perfect vision, or height. One important quality often overlooked by employers is colour vision — an essential requirement for jobs that entail the identification of colour codes, as in many forms of electrical engineering tasks.

Appearance   This criteria is a trap for the unwary. The domed forehead and thick-rimmed spectacles do *not* provide evidence of intelligence. The question of appearance may be important — receptionist, sales jobs and so on — but mistakes are encouraged by

4

interviewers assuming that appearance provides an indication of character, skill, ability, etc. The immaculate suit, impeccable accessories and an upright manner may be the trappings of an idiot.

Intelligence and Initiative   Many job specifications will state 'intelligence' and 'initiative' as essential pre-requisites for the post, and employers have a penchant for mentioning them in recruiting advertisements. The simple fact is that these personal qualities are extremely difficult to identify and measure without recourse to specialised tests. The interviewer may succeed in making a broad-brush and thoroughly subjective assessment, but it will be of little or no value as an aid to *final* assessment of the candidate.

Maturity and Emotional Stability   Assessing these places the interviewer in a cleft stick. Maturity and emotional stability are essential to the acceptance of responsibility — a common and important requirement — but accurate assessment by means of interview is virtually impossible. A candidate's achievement in the past will enable the interviewer to arrive at a subjective judgement — a 'gut-feeling' will probably mislead.

Attitude to Work   The proficient interviewer will probe the candidate's reasons for applying for the job, his aims and intentions at work, and his ambitions — the resulting judgement will provide a valuable indication of the candidate's attitude to work.

Personality   Interviewer, beware. What is personality? Suffice it to say that, by the time we become adults, we display a range of relatively unchanging characteristics — some inherited and some learned along the rocky path of life. The sum and disposition of these traits can be termed 'personality'. The assessment of personality by interview was once summed up by an eminent and very senior naval officer. 'Just ask yourself, m'boy, would you have the fella' in your Mess?' Without recourse to personality tests — and heaven protect the employer who decides to dabble in these murky waters — the poor interviewer may have to follow the admiral's lead.

Hopefully, I have established that the employment interview is, and can only be, a subjective tool of selection. Not only are interviewers different — *people are different.* The interviewer will be faced with candidates who are subject to different kinds of stimulation, who vary widely in kinds and degrees of individual motivation. He will be confronted by people who behave in very diverse ways to achieve a mass of different goals. He will discover different sizes and powers in candidates' physical equipment. In seeking to identify and assess the

5

facts of a candidate's background, he will obtain a glimpse of the myriads of facets which, in sum, represent the character and personality of the individual before him. How best to tackle this complicated and sobering task is the subject of the chapters that follow — cheer up, it can be done.

Self-tutorial (Part One)

A GENERAL QUIZ ON THE PRECEDING CHAPTER

Reader, play the game and attempt this type of quiz by covering all but Question 1 with a piece of paper — and then move the paper down as you proceed from question to question. Remember, no peeping.

Answers	Questions
	1 What is the main purpose of an employment interview?
1 To carry out a comprehensive and accurate background investigation.	2 What, then, is the crux of this process of investigation?
2 To seek out and verify the *facts* of a candidate's background	3 What is an objective selection process?
3 An objective selection process is one in which every judge seeing a performance arrives at exactly the same report.	4 Is the interview an objective process?
4 No — a highly *subjective* process.	5 How may an interviewer lessen the effect of his innate subjectivity?
5 By recognising the characteristics of his own views and prejudices — by being aware of their existence.	6 What is the Halo Error?
6 The error of allowing a general attitude towards the candidate to colour an interviewer's judgement.	7 What is the Mirror-image Error?
7 Be honest. The cardinal sin of selecting the candidate who is most like yourself — and who said *you* were the best thing since sliced bread?	8 What is the danger of the Logical Error?
8 The risk of arriving at similar assessments in respect of qualities that *seem* to be related. Remember the guy who looks like an arch-criminal — but is he?	9 What about the Error of Contrast?
9 Choosing people least like yourself — a measure of pure self-preservation.	10 What is the meaning of 'skill'?

(continued overleaf)

Answers		Questions	
10	The ability to co-ordinate mind and body in the efficient performance of relatively complicated operations.	11	Age may be regarded as a crude measure of — what?
11	Experience — but do not fall headlong into this trap for the unwary.	12	Does the law permit a sex to be specified when advertising a job vacancy?
12	Only in cases where a person's sex can be shown to be a 'GOQ' — genuine occupational qualification.	13	Many interviewers say that they rely heavily on the first impression' gained of a candidate as he enters the interview room. Does this make sense?
13	Apart from an appraisal of the candidate's appearance — *no, it does not make sense.* This is subjective twaddle.	14	If an interviewer is well satisfied that a candidate is mature and emotionally stable — what may he infer?
14	That the candidate is likely to accept, and cope with, elements of responsibility.	15	Does the fact that a candidate has achieved well in the past have any significance to the interviewer?
15	Yes — it provides a *fair* indication that he will achieve well in the future — an achiever is an achiever is an achiever . . .	16	But, surely, it will virtually guarantee that the candidate is a 'safe bet'?
16	Not on your life. The new job could be beyond his level of competency — and there are many other reasons which make it a very 'unsafe bet'.	17	Does colour vision have any significance in the selection process?
17	Most certainly — in electrical engineering, it may be vital to recognise the colour-coding of various components.	18	Have you understood every- thing so far?
18	Yes? Fine — press on. If not — go back ten spaces and start again.		

Self-tutorial (Part Two)

A SPOT OF REVISION — SUBJECTIVITY

The preceding chapter stresses the fact that the interview process is highly subjective. This acute fallibility can be further illustrated by listing some human characteristics and noting how *other* methods fare in trying to measure them objectively:

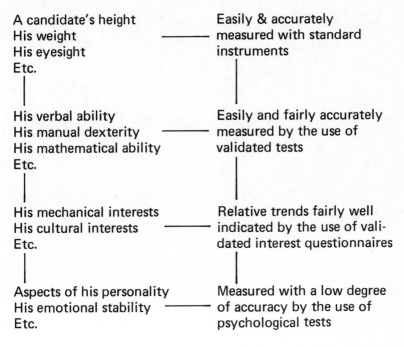

A candidate's height
His weight
His eyesight
Etc.

Easily & accurately
measured with standard
instruments

His verbal ability
His manual dexterity
His mathematical ability
Etc.

Easily and fairly accurately
measured by the use of
validated tests

His mechanical interests
His cultural interests
Etc.

Relative trends fairly well
indicated by the use of validated interest questionnaires

Aspects of his personality
His emotional stability
Etc.

Measured with a low degree
of accuracy by the use of
psychological tests

Now ask yourself the simple question — substitute the interview process for all the above methods, administered by Mr Average, and what have you got? The answer is a ball of chalk!

Let's further think of this;
Weigh what convenience both of time and means
May fit us to our shape: if this should fail,
And that our drift look through our bad performance,
'Twere better not assay'd . . . .

Shakespeare, 'Hamlet, Prince of Denmark'

2

THE ESSENTIAL PRELIMINARIES

The job specification — maligned but mandatory

There is precious little use in interviewing candidates for any job, be it floorsweeper or company executive, unless the requirements of the job have been accurately assessed and the interviewer has a profile of the ideal candidate for the post. It is an unfortunate fact of business life that many employers — in spite of the prolonged efforts of the industrial training boards — still disregard or shy away from *job descriptions* and *job specifications.* Recruitment is essentially a matching process, matching the job with the right man for the job, and effective selection cannot be achieved if the vital preliminaries are ignored or avoided. *There is no short-cut;* the simplest of unskilled jobs should be formally described and, from this detailed description, a job specification prepared. *Remember — the job specification is the blue-print of the successful candidate.*
The main points to be included within a job description are:

1 The job title.
2 The job location.
3 A description of the main function or role of the job.
4 A description of the main duties of the job, e.g. a detailed description of WHAT is done — purpose, scope and duties, responsibilities of the job.

11

The job specification should include:

1 Details of the knowledge and skills required.
2 Details of the education, qualifications and experience needed.
3 Physical qualifications required.
4 Any special requirements – age limits, mobility, etc.

In sum, this is a detailed description of the BEST PERSON for the job – expressed in terms of physical and mental requirements, qualifications and experience.

By carrying out the job specification exercise, you are automatically ensuring a further safeguard against excessive and costly labour turn-over – usually as a result of dismissal for 'incompetence' or 'not fitting in', which are two common excuses offered by employers for their own diabolical selection methods. You will also be sewing the seeds of greater job satisfaction within your workforce. So – try it, it works.

Have you ever thought about your advertising – really thought?

Consider for an instant the aims of effective recruitment advertising:

1 To obtain an *appropriate* response.
2 To provide an adequate description of the post and the relevant terms of employment – expressed in clear, concise and attractive wording.
3 To achieve an overall presentation that enhances the company image.
4 To achieve a correct choice of publication and, within it, to secure the best position, size and timing of the advertisement.

An appropriate response...

'WANTED – YOUNG PERSON TO ASSIST IN GENERAL OFFICE. APPLY TO...' This type of advertisement, seen so often in the classified columns of the provincial press, is likely to produce a spate of applications from youngsters – and, because they must try their luck, oldsters – of all shapes, sizes and calibres. The employer has brought upon himself the unenviable task of weeding out the many applications that are wholly inappropriate, the guys and gals who, given a hundred years, will never acquire the basic skills he requires. Yes, advertising is expensive but so, also, is time.

12

An adequate description...

Quite plainly, an adequate description of the job will help
considerably in obtaining an appropriate response; take special note,
however, of the need for the description to be expressed in clear,
concise and *attractive* terms. Beware of the lazy way out. Try to
avoid the use of such terrible — and often completely false —
clichés such as 'Excellent working conditions', 'Hard-working, happy
team', and so on. The job-seeker will not be overly impressed by this
unimaginative padding — and that is what it is.

Enhance the company image...

The wise employer will recognise that his employment advertising
is a vital part of his corporate identity kit. A poorly designed,
badly worded advertisement — and they are legion — will do
positive harm to the company image. Company image? 'Here we go
again', I hear you say, 'Mine is a small business, just keeping its head
above water. I don't have the time for all these high falutin' textbook
ideals — I just work....' Alright, but spare me a second. Suppose, one
evening, you are enjoying a quiet noggin in your favourite local.
Everything — for a change — is alright with the world until, quite by
chance, you overhear a conversation between those two chaps at the
bar. Would you believe, they are talking about your business!
Naturally, your ears prick up and to your consternation you hear
that they are discussing your firm in most disparaging terms. Not
unnaturally, you feel annoyed. Their remarks are completely without
foundation and, by any standards, they are a slur on your good name.
A slur on your company image. Now, think again of that badly
worded, poorly presented recruiting advertisement. Think of the
number of disparaging comments it will surely provoke — and which
you will not overhear. *Company image....*

Correct choice of publication...

Will a classified ad in the local evening paper produce as many
replies as a similar insertion in the local weekly rag? Is it worth having
a lavish and very costly display advertisement in a prestige national
daily, when a similar and cheaper version in an appropriate
professional journal may well produce more — and better qualified —
applicants? Have you examined the 'pulling potential' of advertisements placed in the growing number of professional tabloid
journals? Or, for that matter, the Town Crier type of publication —

chock-full of ads and distributed free of charge to every household in the area? All too often, little attention is paid to the choice of publication, *and it matters.*

Position, size and timing...

The position a recruiting advertisement occupies on a particular page is an important ingredient in the recipe for success. Your volume of business with the publication concerned will determine whether you are in a position to dictate terms, but do go through the motions of trying to get the best position. A simple rule in this context is: 'Right-hand side — as high as possible'. So — see what you can do. Consider the size of an advertisement by, first, examining the size of those already printed which quote similar requirements to your own. Then — and if you can afford it — decide if you can go one better than your rivals and *design for the additional space.* This does not mean cramming a mass of verbiage into those precious centimetres but, far more effective, ensuring that the punch-lines and headings stand out — catching and holding the eye of the reader.

The timing of an advertisement in a daily publication is of crucial importance. Generally speaking, Mondays and Fridays are the worst days on which to advertise vacancies — when job-seeking morale is either at a low ebb or is swamped by the powerful aphrodisiac of Saturday sport. Again, it is wise to examine a selected newspaper and take careful note of exactly when the advertising peaks and troughs occur.

The lazy path to ineffective advertising...

The vast majority of classified recruiting advertisements are placed by telephone. Little wonder that the results are often calamitious.

> 'Er... is that the classified ad section...? This is so-and-so....
> I want to place the following small ad in your job vacancies
> column — yes, I'll read it to you.... Er... Wanted... Filing Clerk —
> put that in big letters, please.... A vacancy exists for a school-
> leaver to, er... undertake filing duties in our office — no, make
> that general office.... The successful applicant — what? Oh,
> yes, a full-stop after general office. Where was I — the
> successful applicant will have — no, possess — a flair — yes,
> F-L-A-I-R — for, er... neatness and accuracy. Applications
> should be made in writing to — and I suppose the name and
> address should be in bold print? Right, well — it'll be Mr J.T. —
> no, J for John — Allison. That's two L's and one S. We'd better
> have the company name in biock capitals — Plastisocks
> Limited... That's P-L-A-S-T....'

14

By telephoning his requirements, the advertiser has placed himself entirely at the mercy of whoever takes the call — and one has only to scan the classified columns to see the outcome of such a gamble. Lack of time is invariably a poor excuse for such misplaced faith. *All recruiting ads should be order in writing and should be accompanied by concise instructions regarding size, layout and choice of print.*

The immoral practice of 'blinkering'...

The pernicious habit of advertising under a box number continues to flourish. The employer who resorts to this cloak of anonymity usually does so for a variety of reasons:

1   The firm enjoys a bad name in the neighbourhood.
2   Some poor soul is currently occupying the post being advertised — and will get the quick bullet when a successor is found.
3   For some dark and sinister reason, the firm wishes to keep its employees in ignorance of the vacancy.

Let there be no mistake, the intelligent job-seeker tends to regard such advertisements with a degree of suspicion, and rightly so. Many discerning people will not respond to a box number and, quite probably, this group will include the best person for the job.

Which brings me to that dreaded phrase: 'Salary negotiable'. Again, the thinking job-seeker is immediately aware that the firm is trying to obtain someone 'on the cheap' or, just as likely, that existing employees are to be kept in ignorance of the rate for the new post. I wish I could be hopeful and forecast that the practice will change, but it is probably here to stay. Unfortunately, it is too easy to quote the 'exigencies of business' as a trite excuse for such parsimony or downright immorality.

And so we come to short-listing

While a growing number of employers are utilising nicely printed and even well designed application forms (of which more anon), there remain very many hardy souls who still require applicants to go through the business of producing the dreaded *curriculum vitae* (CV) — and, by thus sticking to a fairly down-at-heel tradition, create for themselves a whole welter of problems. Consider, if you will, the 'hand-made' application in the context of the short-listing process, and picture the average scene. Faced with a number — which can be very large — of applications of all shapes and sizes, the poor old short-lister commences his task of sorting out the wheat from the chaff. First, a superbly confident riffle through the pile, then another — and, with rapidly draining confidence, another . . . . Odd words and phrases, examples of handwriting and typing (some beautiful, some execrable) strike his meandering eye — as, indeed, does a bewildering variety of formats, styles and presentations. But the name of the game is short-listing and, since something has to be done, the hapless selector will usually start by placing odd applications to one side. This one looks good for that reason — this application deserves further attention for another reason . . . . Very quickly, the manager's desk is covered with motley groups of papers, and he's completely lost. On returning to the first 'pick-out' pile, he finds he has no idea what prompted the segregation, and so the wretched business continues! This description may seem larger than life, but the hard fact remains that the task of short-listing is seldom carried out in a logical manner — and probably never if the advertised vacancy has produced a crop of individually composed CVs. The inevitable result is that much time is wasted and, even worse, there is the chance that an entirely suitable application will be discarded.

The golden rules for effective short-listing...

1 Enjoy, whenever possible, the great advantage of standardised AND VALID application forms. At the very least, the use of a printed application form will ensure that the personal history of each candidate is presented within an identical, pre-designed format — and comparisons between, for instance, applicants' qualifications can then be made with the maximum of ease and efficiency. *Essential details will spring to the eye.* However, it should be remembered that the design of application forms is a crafty art in itself, and not a task to be handed with gay abandon to a little girl secretary for completion between letters. Putting it bluntly, if a company's *tour de force* poses peanut-type questions, it will evoke monkey-type answers — see the Appendix, Further Aids to Efficient Selection, for a few tips.

2 Use — and be familiar with — the job specification. Remember, like it or not, it is the blue-print of the successful candidate.

3 Interpret the data correctly. Here are a few tips on interpretation:

Handwriting Unless the needs of the post dictate a skill in copperplate — forward, Mr Scrooge! — do not be inclined to reject the untidy writer out of hand. Too many employers tend to condemn bad handwriting, particularly in the case of applicants for office posts — yet they may seldom lift a pen during the course of their work. Bad spelling and improper grammar are certainly indicators of something — but, think on't, some of our finest brains cannot spell to save their lives.

Details of examinations passed That which a candidate *omits* when completing his application may be significant. A statement of passes attained in 'O' Level English Literature, Art and History will, in many cases, indicate failures in English Language, Mathematics and so on. The reasons for such failures are of great importance to the selector, but one cannot expect the applicant to catalogue them for his benefit. Remember that pass grades may also be omitted if, in the view of the applicant, they will damage his case.

Job titles   Many companies tend to feed their corporate ego by allotting grandiose titles to comparatively minor jobs. A company with which I was once associated had, as an off-shoot to its main activity, an involvement in car hire. The car hire section boasted a staff of one, a clerk-receptionist — but the company insisted that this chap's title was Car Hire Manager. One could hardly blame him if, when applying for another job, he entered the 'official title' on his application form. It behoves the selector to look closely at job titles, particularly if it is possible to do this at the short-listing stage.

Typing and shorthand skills   Many office staff are accepted for jobs for which they are subsequently found to be over- or under-qualified in terms of their typing or shorthand skills. The selector must be familiar with the exact requirements for such posts — it's back to that specification again — and, of course, he must be able to interpret an applicant's stated qualifications in the light of these requirements. (See the self-tutorial section at the end of this chapter for some helpful details.)

Service in HM Forces   The people who design application forms — and I would very much like to meet some of them — are fond of including a separate section for detailing any service in the armed forces. All too often, however, candidates are merely required to enter the service concerned, the branch or trade, dates and the applicant's rank on leaving. Selectors should insist that application forms provide an adequate opportunity to highlight their service experience, in terms of duties and training. Now, short-listers, there comes a note of caution. The armed forces of today are very different to those of yesteryear. The standards required of personnel of all grades are extremely high and the many training courses and activities reflect this demand. In fact, the average serviceman will be streets ahead of his civilian counterpart from a training point of view — particularly in the field of administration. So, when interpreting service histories, bear this fact in mind. Those short-listers who retain painful or nostalgic memories of their service days should remember that it was a long time ago — and, in some cases, a *very* long time ago.

Hobbies and sparetime interests   This section of the application form can be very revealing. A comprehensive investigation of a

17

candidate's background must plainly include the one-third of his life which is not taken up with work or sleep. The selector will require to know whether the man's horizons extend beyond the daily grind of earning money and sitting at home with the television. The interpretation of stated hobbies and interests is essential, but must be undertaken with care:

a   The big question — is that which is stated *true,* or is it window-dressing? Chapter 6 deals with the issue of fibbers, liars and damned liars.
b   Are the activities listed merely passive pursuits? The hardy perennial, 'reading' — sometimes listed by wily candidates as 'literature' — should be virtually discounted, *unless* the candidate supplies further details.
c   As a rule, candidates who supply fulsome explanations of spare-time interests, as opposed to mere lists of activities, are usually lively practitioners in those activities. The short-lister is, or should be, looking for the applicant with some fire in his belly — and spare-time interests may provide the clue.

The curriculum vitae   If the short-lister is unlucky and standard application forms have not been used, he will be faced with a series of hand-composed documents. These will range from ill-written, untidy scraps of paper to virtual masterpieces of biographical art. The best advice I can offer is to study the 'rules of the game' as seen by a candidate who is determined to submit a winning *curriculum vitae (CV):*

a   He will ensure that his CV is type-written and, regardless of the extent of his search for employment, *never* in stencilled or photostat form.
b   He will ensure that the CV is produced on A4 or foolscap paper, and that the layout is crisp and pleasing to the eye. He may employ a further trick of the application game and utilise paper of a distinctive colour or quality — thereby ensuring that his CV will stand out in the short-lister's pile. Think about this one; a CV typed on best quality paper, say, of a rich cream hue *would* get picked out.
c   *He will tailor his CV to the requirements of the post.* Unhampered by the lack of space on a printed application form, he will ensure that descriptions of past activities are, as far as possible, in keeping with what the short-lister will wish to see.
d   He will ensure that his covering letter is brief and succinct — merely an introduction to his *tour de force.*

e   His CV will never contain 'flannel'. Such statements as 'I am
confident that I would succeed in this post because I enjoy
dealing with people...' are not for this brand of applicant.

Acknowledging applications

The worst and most common sin committed by would-be
employers is the failure to acknowledge applications promptly. The
habit of allowing the pile to accumulate over a period of days — or,
would you believe, weeks — without the courtesy of acknowledge-
ment is inexcusable. A short note, or even a postcard — containing
thanks and the statement that the application is receiving attention —
is the essential chore, to be implemented by return of post. Then,
once short-listing is complete, attention should be turned to the
question of rejection letters and invitations to interview.

The rejection letter

Some letters of rejection read more like a judgement from the
county court. Such curt brush-offs do no good at all; the letters
should be couched in kind terms and, shades of company image,
should be a good advertisement for the firm. The aim of the exercise
is to convince the unlucky applicant that someone *has* examined
his application in depth — that he has been fairly treated. It is a
moot point whether, in trying to be kind, employers should add
that hackneyed line, '... your application will be placed on file, de
dah, de dah...'. It is usually a false statement and, as such, is not
really playing the game. The final act of kindness is to make the
letter informal: 'Dear Mr Brown' and 'Yours sincerely...'.

The invitation to interview

Yes, invitation.... No useful purpose is served by sending a letter
which is akin to a summons to an inquisition. Again, the invitation
should be couched in informal terms and should contrive to show
an element of interest in the candidate — not to the extent, however, that he thinks the job is in the bag. The letter should always
contain a statement to the effect that, if the appointment is
inconvenient, so-and-so can be contacted for an alternative
arrangement. Companies worth their salt will always reimburse
candidates' reasonable travelling expenses and this should also be
mentioned.

Self-tutorial (Part One)

A GENERAL QUIZ ON THE PRECEDING CHAPTER

Answers   **Questions**

                                               1   What is the essential difference
                                               between a *job description* and a
                                               job specification?

1   A *job description* is a detailed   2   What are the essential
observation of WHAT is done,   ingredients for a successful
a job specification is a detailed   employment ad?
description of the BEST PERSON
for the job.

2   (a) Accurate and attractive text.   3   How should employments ads
    (b) Eye-catching design.   always be ordered?
    (c) The right publication.
    (d) Correct timing.
    (e) Adequate size.
    (f) Best position on page.
    And a slice of luck.

3   In writing — NEVER by   4   How do standardised
telephone.   application forms help the
     short-lister?

4   By enabling him to pinpoint   5   What is a possible disadvantage
and compare data easily and   of standardised application
quickly.   forms?

5   The stricture of limited space.   6   What, then, is the possible
Candidates may be unable to   disadvantage of the
provide adequate information   curriculum vitae?
(i.e. duties and responsibilities),
and the short-lister's task will
be all the more difficult.

6   Not so much the obvious fact   7   What should happen
that information will be   immediately an application
presented in a non-standard   is received?
form, but that the candidate
may salt his production with
subjective material; simply,
'flannel'.

7   It should be acknowledged.

8   To notify rejection in kindly
    and courteous terms; to
    convince the candidate that he
    has received full and fair
    treatment from a first-class
    organisation.

9   Start by reading Chapter 6.

8   What are the essential aims
    of the rejection letter?

9   How do I deal with doubtful
    information?

Self-tutorial (Part Two)

A BRIEF GUIDE TO SHORTHAND AND TYPING SPEEDS

Shorthand

Under 80 wpm   Look closely at any applicant in this category — the qualification is poor.

80 wpm   The speed one would expect in a junior applicant — much will depend on the volume of work inherent in the post. Think carefully.

Around 100 wpm   The very average secretary's speed.

120-130 wpm   A first-class speed — does the volume of work justify it?

Above 130 wpm   The speed of a shorthand specialist. Beware of taking on someone who is over-qualified for the job. This could lead to intense dissatisfaction and early resignation.

Typing

25 wpm   The speed of an office junior who, to improve, needs day release to attend further training.

35 wpm   Average proficiency — remember to check the quality of the applicant's work.

50 wpm or over   Very superior typing ability which reflects mental alertness — again, check that the applicant is not over-qualified for the job concerned.

Self-tutorial (Part Three)

Here is a fairly typical curriculum vitae — examine it and compile a list of the points which, in your view, should be given special attention during the selection process. Compare your results with the representative list which follows the CV.

CURRICULUM VITAE

John Reginald SMITH

25 The Coppice
East Formby
Hazeldene
Bucks HA2 5NN

Married — with three dependents
Date of birth — 10 August 1936   *Tel:* Hazeldene 44321

Career to date

Nov 73 — Date	Personnel Manager to J.R. Franklin (Plastics) Ltd. Responsible for all personnel matters for 1,200 employees, including selection and recruitment, wage/salary admin., industrial relations. Salary on leaving: £4250 p.a. Reason for leaving — to better my position.
Jan 73 — Sep 73	Personnel Officer with H.G. Developments Ltd. Responsible for all personnel matters for 650 employees. Salary on leaving: £3000 p.a. Reason for leaving — to improve my career.
Oct 68 — Jan 73	Grants Officer with the Road Transport Industry Training Board. Responsible for training advice to companies in Board's scope in Sussex & Surrey area. Salary on leaving: £2225 p.a. Reason for leaving — to enter industry.
Sep 56 — Sep 68	Administrative Officer with British Railways, Southern Region. General administrative responsibilities. Salary on leaving: £1150 p.a. Reason for leaving — to better my position.
Jun 52 — Aug 54	Shop assistant — Mungles Bookshops Ltd.

Education

1947 — 1952   Hazeldene Grammar School — School
                   Certificate in English Language, Art, Office
                   Practice, Organisation and Administration.

Qualifications

Associate Member Institution of Training Officers
Pass with Distinction NEBSS Course

Hobbies

Bob-sleighing, travel, literature, DIY.

Health

Good

Points requiring investigation

1   Smith has been a trifle reticent concerning his dependents. The
     interviewer will need to probe this area, e.g. an aged grand-
     parent living at home might well restrict Smith's personal
     mobility.

2   He has entered the word 'date' in connection with his last or
     current job. It is not clear whether Smith has actually left the
     company. If, indeed, he has quitted this job, his stated reason
     for leaving must be examined — for he had no alternative
     employment arranged. Was he sacked?

3   Smith has supplied a poor description of his job responsibilities
     in his last post — a vital area for investigation.

4   He has omitted to provide employer's addresses — this need not
     be sinister, but the interviewer will certainly need these details.

5   There is a gap of some weeks between Smith's last and penulti-
     mate jobs. Does this lend strength to his stated reason for
     leaving H.G. Developments — I think not.

6   Did Smith actually improve his career after leaving H.G. Developments?

7   He gives no details of his National Service — but there is a significant gap in his employment history from 1954 to 1956. Did National Service account for this, or is there a more sinister reason?

8   There were no School Certificates in Office Practice or 'Org and Admin' — is this an attempt at flannel?

9   Smith's AMITO qualification was presumably obtained when he was with the Training Board — yet he makes no mention of passing an approved training officers' course. Certainly, the AMITO was obtained without examination.

10   Where and when did Smith pass the NEBSS Supervisors' Course?

11   Bob-sleighing? How did he manage to afford that? *Did* he do it? Look at the remaining hobbies with a jaundiced eye — they are the infernal trio.

Salus populi suprema est lex.
The good of the people is the chief law.

Cicero (106-43 BC), 'De Legibus'

3

THE INTERVIEWING ENVIRONMENT

'Well, if you ask me, any applicant for a job expects competition. The interviewer is tasked with picking the best of the bunch and, frankly, shouldn't pussyfoot his way through the procedure. It's an adult world and candidates for any job must be put to the test. For instance, why not keep 'em waiting for a bit before wheeling them in for interview? And — when a chap does sit in front of you and finds that the sun is in his eyes — why not wait to see if he has the gumption to do anything about it? I believe that this kind of thing puts the candidate on his mettle from the start. Interviewing isn't a friendly tea-party or a talk with the vicar — it's a serious test and everything about it should be devoted to the one task of picking out the wheat from the damned chaff. I've very little time for the textbook idealists — I say put every applicant through the hoop. Test 'em until they drop and then test 'em again.'

These words were uttered by an eminently successful businessman who, in his time, has put many candidates through his much-loved interviewing hoop. The significant and alarming fact — despite our hero's success in business — is that this militant approach to selection is *utterly wrong*. The purpose of this chapter is to persuade and convince you, the reader, that such views are untenable; the interview environment must never be allowed to form a backdrop to a process of inquisition. So — let us examine those conditions which have a vital effect on the validity of an interview and which, in sum, comprise this much-abused question of environment.

27

The reception of candidates

There is one aspect of interview administration which, although positively Dickensian in origin, is still widely used — particularly in the field of education. It is that pernicious habit of requiring all candidates to turn up for interview at the same time, regardless of the timing of individual sessions. The unfortunate group spends a prolonged period of stressful inactivity, whilst each member is interviewed in turn. Timid folk suffer at the hands of the more ebullient candidates and those who are last on the interview schedule undergo a quite inexcusable agony of suspense. The emergence of the final candidate from the inner sanctum is usually the signal for further delay and the group, painfully aware that the moment of truth is drawing nigh, wait with baited breath for the name of the lucky applicant to be announced. At long last, the selected individual is invited to return to the high altar and the dispirited remainder are free to contrive a dignified exit. Sadly, many organisations continue to practise this needless and archaic form of interview administration, with utter disregard for the candidates' feelings and, as I shall explain, to the detriment of good selection.

The timing of interviews is crucial to the process and there are a number of vital considerations to be taken into account:

1   Candidates should *never* be allowed to meet. There is nothing to be gained and much to be lost by permitting an applicant to 'weigh up the opposition'. Not only will he form premature — and probably inaccurate — views on his chances of success, but he will be in a position to compare notes on the interviewer's displayed weaknesses and techniques — something to be avoided like the plague.
2   The duration of each interview is bound to vary. The interviewer who is constrained by the dictates of a rigid timetable will find it virtually impossible to conduct fully effective and searching interviews. Appointments should reflect the need for flexibility and, most important, must provide adequate time to enable a formal assessment of each candidate to be made immediately after each session.
3   Appointment times should always take account of candidates' travelling needs and, whenever possible, the dictates of their current employment. A man's employer is usually unaware that he is seeking an alternative job and it may be difficult for the candidate to obtain time off to attend for interview during his working hours. 'What — is the tail wagging the dog?', do I hear you say? Come off it — there are such things as

evening and Saturday morning interviews, and you are looking for a chap with loyalty.

4   Waiting time should be kept to a minimum. Kicking one's heels in anxious anticipation of the call to 'please come this way' is distinctly akin to an appointment with the dentist, and how many of us enjoy visiting the dentist?

Responsible, *thinking* organisations will always ensure that candidates are greeted on arrival by a competent receptionist, *who will know exactly what is going on.* The quietly efficient and pleasant reception of candidates is not only an act of courtesy, but also constitutes an invaluable advertisement for the company in general. Waiting areas should be made as attractive as possible, with an adequate supply of literature, preferably not dog-eared remnants of a bygone age. It is a good idea to action a candidate's claim for travelling expenses prior to the interview — this, again, will impress him with the general efficiency of the organisation.

The interview room

'Come into my parlour', said the spider to the fly...

Interviews are usually conducted in the office of the executive concerned; very few organisations seem able, or inclined, to set aside special accommodation for interviewing purposes. The results are often little short of disastrous. One company's concept of suitable office accommodation varies widely from that of another, and interviews suffer accordingly. Rightly or wrongly, I consider it a futile exercise to describe the ideal interviewing room in glowing detail, when such accommodation will be beyond the wildest dreams of so many struggling interviewers. In an effort to be practical, I will attempt to highlight the main aspects of this very important facet of the interview environment — and, at the same time, urge all inter-viewers to use their native cunning, if not the firm's money, to bring about any necessary improvements.

First, however, it is necessary to dispose of the devil's disciples — those positively evil interviewers who believe that even the interview accommodation must form part and parcel of their selection procedure.

Variations on a theme of chairs

1   The first trick — a Machiavellian device if there ever was one —

29

consists of having two chairs available for the candidate's use; a hard, upright version and a comfortable armchair. The so-called interviewer receives the poor victim and, with bated breath, waits to see which chair he will elect to use. Having witnessed the great moment, our errant and amateur psychologist then proceeds to attach a deep significance to the candidate's choice — a significance which colours his entire judgement of the applicant.

2   The second trick in this armoury of nonsense entails the use of a chair which is so low that the candidate can barely see over his own knees, let alone over the interview desk. The inquisitor, observing the candidate from on high, rubs his hands with glee and awaits a reaction from the victim. Presumably, a request by the candidate to change his seat will be viewed as conclusive evidence of strength of character, whilst a lack of reaction will serve to convince the interviewer that he is dealing with a timid wretch, unworthy of selection.

3   Finally, there is the ridiculous business of seating the candidate on an office chair with restrictive wooden arms. In this instance, the chap is watched like a hawk to see if he permits himself the sybaritic luxury of leaning on the arms or, instead, sits like a vestal virgin with hands in lap, awaiting his doom. Needless to say, both postures signify matters of great import to the sagacious inquisitor!

The 'powers of observation' trick

There are a number of Colonel Blimp-like interviewers who enjoy hazy memories, or misconceptions, of the manner in which service selection boards did their stuff in the good old days of the Second World War — and the 'powers of observation' gambit is a hardy perennial of their stock-in-trade. At some point in the interview, the candidate will be invited to '... kindly wait in the outer office whilst I make a telephone call ...'. When recalled to the interviewer's presence, the victim will be asked some damn-fool question — like, 'Tell me, how many pictures did you happen to see on the walls of my secretary's office?' The nature of the unfortunate candidate's reply will enable Colonel Blimp, in his infinite wisdom, to pronounce on the chap's powers of observation.

The repertoire of these interviewers-cum-tricksters seems endless. Their fascination for using the interview environment as a vehicle for devious and thoroughly invalid testing is matched only by their supreme vanity in believing that they can interpret the results. Such gimmicks — for that is what they are — are worthless, misleading and utterly reprehensible.

Desk or no desk?

Should there be a desk between interviewer and candidate? There is little doubt that the use of a desk places a stamp of formality on the proceedings; but is this strictly necessary? Whilst it may be desirable to conduct some interviews in formal vein — say, the selection of junior employees — the face-to-face confrontation over the desk is not always the best mode of approach. There will be many occasions when a less formal situation, utilising easy chairs and a coffee table, will vastly enhance the overall productivity of the interview — *and it is productivity with which we are concerned.* Both participants will be more relaxed and there is certainly more of a chance that the session will be conducted as a purposeful and steered conversation. In sum, the interviewer will have ensured that the '... and when did you last see your father?' syndrome is absent from the session, and a more mature candidate will give of his best. But there is a snag! Many interviewers take positive refuge behind the comforting presence of a desk and, if required to perform without this castle wall, would be very ill-at-ease. However, it is to be hoped that such interviewers, especially having read this book, will recognise that their fears are groundless and usually stem from an ignorance of interviewing techniques.

One thing is certain; if a desk is used, it must be cleared of all extraneous papers, files and so on. A cluttered desk is a sure sign of inefficiency on the part of the interviewer and usually an indication of insecurity — 'I must always look busy and then I'm fireproof'. It is also a bad advertisement for the company; so — let neatness be the order of the day. But, if a desk is to be clear of papers, what about the business of taking notes? This is a fairly vexed question and it must be admitted that opinions are divided on the issue of whether or not notes should be taken during an interview. My personal view is that, with the exception of brief jottings in order to record absolutely vital dates, etc., notes should *not* be taken in the presence of the candidate. Using the methods outlined in Chapter 7, the reader will find that, given practice, he will be able to complete a thoroughly comprehensive appraisal of any candidate, without recourse to copious note-taking during the interview. Remember, also, that an interview which is punctuated with long periods of silence whilst the interviewer composes a mini-biography is hardly conducive to a smooth discussion. But more of this anon.

The interview room in general

The golden rule is simply that the interview room — be it cupboard under the stairs or palatial executive suite — *must be distraction-free.* This means a little more than merely ensuring that undue noise does not intrude upon the interview — which, of course, it mustn't. The candidate should not be seated in such a manner that the sun shines directly into his eyes, and his chair should be moderately comfortable. Visual distractions — say, the view through the window of a busy street or the sight of another office through a glass partition — must be kept to a minimum. Bearing in mind the sad fact that so many of us are not blessed with decent offices, it is wise to note that *nothing distracts a candidate more than tatty surroundings.* A poorly appointed office will provide an interviewee with a definite and adverse impression of the organisation as a whole. Remember the last time you visited an untidy, down-at-heel office — did it not colour your views?

Interruptions

The interviewing process is beset with gremlins and one particularly adroit hobgoblin is clearly tasked with ensuring that all interviews are interrupted as often as possible. Once a session is under way, the telephone — having remained silent for hours — will ring incessantly and visitors will descend upon the office from all points of the compass. Make no mistake, such interruptions are fatal and must not be allowed to disrupt the proceedings. Apart from creating havoc with the interview plan, interruptions provide the candidate with a heaven-sent opportunity to assess his position and tailor his strategy accordingly. Those interviewers who are lucky enough to possess a secretary should make absolutely certain that Girl or Boy Friday guards the uninterrupted sanctity of the interview. Less fortunate individuals should take the simple precautions of instructing the switchboard not to pass calls until notified — remember to give the all-clear when you are finished — and, most important, display a notice on their office door, 'Interview in Progress — Keep Out'.

To smoke or not to smoke?

The question, 'Should a candidate be allowed to smoke?', is often posed by thoughtful interviewers. Whilst there will always be the odd candidate who, immediately he is seated, will fish out his cigarettes and proceed to scatter ash without a care in the world and certainly without being asked, the vast majority are well-mannered. One thing is sure; if a candidate is a smoker, the interview is the one time when he will probably be in dire need of a puff or two. The kindly interviewer, particularly if he is a smoker, will issue an invitation to light up and will ensure that an ashtray is within easy reach. But, since there are many of us who cannot abide the habit, the answer to the question must remain one of personal preference. I cannot see much justification in permitting the very young or junior applicants to smoke during the interview, but there may be a case for extending the courtesy to older and more senior candidates.

* * *

To sum up, the environment in which the interview is conducted will have a profound effect on the outcome of the process. If a candidate, by virtue of the general environment, is made to feel completely at ease, he will naturally give of his best — and the interviewer's task will be that much more pleasant. Conversely, a bad interview environment will almost certainly induce the applicant to form a poor opinion of the organisation — an opinion which he will not keep to himself. Go to it — there is always this particular room for improvement!

* * *

The interviewing environment — an employers' checklist

1   Has the person responsible for the reception of candidates received a thorough briefing? For example:
   a   If inexperienced, has the receptionist been reminded of the paramount need for a pleasant and efficient manner?
   b   Have you provided reception with an appointments list?
   c   Will each candidate be informed of the interviewer's name and function within the company?
   d   Is the waiting area presentable — literature (including literature on the company), ashtrays?
   e   Does the receptionist know that candidates should be *offered* assistance with any general queries?
   f   Have arrangements been made for the completion — and payment — of expense claims; is sufficient petty cash available for this?
   g   Are timetables, etc., available for the planning of candidates' return trips?

2   In compiling your appointments list, have you allowed for
candidates' needs, e.g.
- *a*   Those who will have spent the previous night in a hotel —
early morning appointments?
- *b*   Those who will have a long journey to your office — early
afternoon appointments?

3   Does the appointments list cater adequately for:
- *a*   Flexibility of interview duration?
- *b*   Adequate time for post-interview appraisal?

4   Candidates may telephone the office for some reason. Have you
supplied the telephonist with a copy of the appointment list?

5   Have you decided whether the interviews will be formal or
informal?

6   Have you checked that:
- *a*   Candidates' seating is adequate with regard to comfort,
sunlight, etc?
- *b*   Extraneous noise is minimised?
- *c*   The office is clean and tidy?
- *d*   Your desk is clear?
- *e*   It carries your name-plate?
- *f*   The telephone is cut off?
- *g*   If necessary, your 'Do Not Disturb' notice is in position?
- *h*   You are familiar with the candidates' written applications?

'The only way to escape misrepresentation is never commit oneself to any critical judgement that makes an impact — that is, never say anything.

F.R. Leavis, 'The Great Tradition'

4

THE NITTY-GRITTY OF EFFECTIVE INTERVIEWING

There was once, or so the story goes, a certain Royal Navy Selection Board. Tasked with selecting the cream of British youth for cadet-ships at the RN College, the board members were an impressive band. The President, an Admiral of great distinction, was flanked by three senior officers and a bowler-hatted emissary from the Admiralty. Before this august presence there sat a young lad who, at the time our story opens, had already succeeded in answering a number of questions with refreshing candour and obvious intelligence. The Admiral groped in his mental ditty-box for the next question.

'Tell me, my lad', he asked, 'Have any members of your family served in the Royal Navy?'

'Yes indeed, sir', the lad replied. 'My father is a Captain, at present commanding HMS So-and-so, and my grandfather retired from the Service some years ago. I believe he was Flag Officer, Glasgow, when he retired.'

'Capital, capital', said the Admiral, pleased that his question had produced such a response. 'It helps us to know that you have a Service background. By the way, have any other of your relatives followed their example?'

'Yes, sir. My brother is a Lieutenant serving in the Far East and I have a cousin in the Royal Australian Navy. I suppose it was really my great-grandfather who started it all — Admiral So-and-so — he served for some forty years.'

'Absolutely splendid!' the Admiral beamed with pleasure. Then his face hardened. 'Now, young man, think carefully — *why do you wish to join the Royal Navy?*'

It probably never happened — or did it? In taking a further look-see at the fallibility of interviewing as a tool of selection, we have to recognise that this type of question crops up with monotonous regularity. Interviewers seem to place singular weight on candidates' replies to the question, 'Why do you wish to join this company?' If asked, an interviewer will usually explain that a candidate's response provides a valuable insight into his motivation and personality. Well, does it?'

'Why do you wish to join this company, Mr. Brown?'
'Well, as I said earlier, this particular job aroused my interest as soon as I read your advertisement. My qualifications meet your requirements and I'm confident that my past experience would enable me to succeed in the post. If I may say, your company is a leader in its particular field and — from the little I know of your marketing philosophy — I think it will stay that way. Mr Williams, I'm sure that, if I'm selected for the job, the company would derive a fair benefit from my efforts. I'm equally confident that the company, for its part, would ensure that my work received adequate recognition. This is a difficult question to answer — I hope that I've gone a little way in providing a reply.'
'Yes — I see ....'
'In a nutshell, Mr Williams, I wish to work for a successful and go-ahead organisation and contribute towards that success. Your company is my choice.'

What would your reaction be to such a reply?

Splendid effort — not only expresses himself well, but talks sense into the bargain ....

Bumptious creeper ....

He'd make a good second-hand car salesman — but I want an accountant ....

Self-opinionated, but maybe someone with a bit of push ....

Ah, he's taken the trouble to find out something about the company — I like that ....

Biggest load of flannel I've ever heard ....

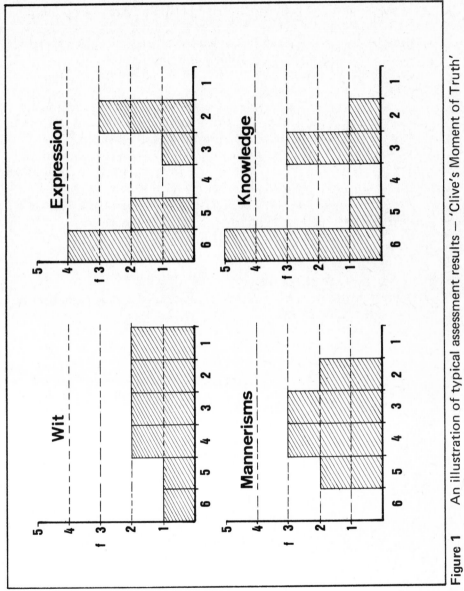

Figure 1   An illustration of typical assessment results — 'Clive's Moment of Truth'

Speaks frankly — obviously knows what he wants ....

The important point is that any reaction — whatever form it may take — is entirely subjective. For the great majority of us, such judgements will be little more than educated guesses — and this is a very hard pill to swallow. We go through life making snap assessments of people — 'I like him' — 'I think he's a nasty piece of work' — and then someone has the utter gall to say that this lifelong practice is mere guesswork? Let me tell you about Clive's Moment of Truth ....

Not so long ago, I had occasion to deliver a lecture to a group of headmasters. This in itself was a trifle foolhardy, since an audience of headmasters is easily the worst in the world. However, it had to be done and I decided to profit from the occasion by conducting a hackneyed but useful little experiment in appraisal. Each headmaster was issued with a very simple rating form on which, by use of 1-to-6 rating scales, he was invited to assess my lecturing prowess under four headings:

Wit

Powers of expression

Mannerisms

Knowledge of the subject

At the conclusion of the lecture, the assessments were gathered in from this erudite audience — and the collated results are shown in Figure 1. Remembering that each headmaster observed the same chap, heard the same words and saw the same mannerisms — look at the outcome. Where is the consensus of opinion? Whose judgement is the correct judgement? The pill *must* be swallowed; we are not capable of making objective assessments of this nature — so why attempt to make a subjective interview process even more subjective? Let me remind you of the golden rule: *the purpose of the interview is to carry out a comprehensive and accurate background investigation — to seek out and verify the facts of past achievement and failure.* Get to it — don't bother to ask the chap why he wishes to join the company. Establish from his past performance whether he will be a credit to the firm if he does join! This is fallible enough; don't make it worse.

The group or board interview

The group or board interview can be effective, but very seldom is. One reason for this is that three — or whatever — ill-trained interviewers attempting to work together as a cohesive selection filter can be infinitely worse than any solo practitioner. Let us examine a typical example of an interview board in the field of further of education:

Members   A county education official
                Two college governors
                The college principal

The Board's Task   To interview short-listed candidates and select a new member of the college staff

For the purposes of this illustration, we must subject the worthy members of the Board to some close inspection. What, if any, are the attitudes and possible interactions which may have a prejudicial effect on the selection process?

Governor A, who happens to be a Tory Councillor, cannot stand Governor B, who gives every appearance of being a red-hot Communist and who manages to hold up and disrupt proceedings at every governors' meeting. Governor A is determined that his undesirable colleague will not prevent justice being done on *this* important occasion. Governor A has met the college staff *en masse* at various sherry parties and has noted, with much concern, the apparent deterioration of standards within some sections of the establishment. He finds it difficult to distinguish between many of the lecturers and the students they teach — wildly unkept hair, a plethora of scruffy jeans and unpolished footwear, an air of casual disregard for any form of authority. Governor A is at a loss to understand why the Principal — a competent and well-qualified man in his field — makes no apparent effort to correct the situation. One thing is certain, Governor A — who has interviewed more candidates for jobs than he cares to remember — will not allow the current Board to recruit yet another cowboy to the teaching scene at this college.

Governor B, a man of Socialist leanings, has 'come up the hard way' — and is now a successful executive in life assurance. A swift thinker and a proponent of the hard-sell technique, he cannot understand why that pompous idiot, Governor A, has been recruited to the Board. In fact, he feels that the old fool should have given up the reins long ago and let some fresh blood have a crack of the whip. He is fairly certain that the Principal shares his opinion of Governor A but that, in allowing him full rein to blunder on at every opportunity, the Principal is intent on buttering his political toast. Governor B has two clear aims where this new appointment is concerned. He intends that the best applicant — and he has an exact conception of the ideal man for the job — will win the post, and he is going to confound Governor A at every juncture. Sooner or later, people have got to realise that Governor A is 'past it' and he, Governor B, is the man to convince them.

The Principal is still smarting from the effects of a disastrous Press release by the County Education Department on the threat of teacher redundancies. He has been told that the Deputy Education Officer — the chap on this interview board — was primarily responsible for the Press release and he is not impressed by the man's apparent lack of very basic judgement. He is also aware that the DEO switched to education management very early in his career and, as a consequence, lacks any form of recent experience 'at the sharp end' of the profession. It would be true to say that the Principal has a natural antipathy towards anyone from the ivory tower of County Hall playing an active part in the task of selecting his staff. He regards himself with some justification as the only 'professional' on the interviewing board and, to this end, is anxious that his questioning technique reflects his standing. He does not enjoy the formal interviewing process and would much rather have long, informal discussions with the candidates concerned. He is aware that his manner becomes stilted and somewhat cold when participating in a board interview, and he wishes that he could become more relaxed.

The Principal regards Governor A as a quite pleasant gentleman of the old school, a man who lends presence to the Board of Governors and who wields considerable political influence in favour of the college. He is bound to admit, however, that Governor A has some rather old-fashioned ideas and these tend to create difficulties where the selection of staff is concerned. The Principal admires — or is it envies? — Governor B for his forceful and persuasive manner. He is well aware that Governor B would be a formidable enemy and he is thankful that the man seems to have the interests of the college at heart. He is not entirely happy, however, that neither Governor has sufficient knowledge and experience of the teaching world to enable them to choose the right candidate for the job.

The Principal also faces a difficult situation. He has an existing member of staff who, in terms of qualifications and service, merits selection for the new post. He is aware that several external candidates may well outshine this man when they are interviewed — and he has done his best to pave the way in advance, by having private words with the two governors. Governor A asked for a description of the staff member concerned and then remarked that he remembered the man, and could not totally agree with the Principal's comments. Governor B appeared to accept the Principal's approach, but seemed disinclined to form any opinion until he had seen the external candidates.

The county education official — the DEO — has given little thought to his colleagues on the interviewing board. He regards the Principal as a pleasant enough chap, good at his job and apparently devoted to his college. He is inclined to make an undue fuss from time to time at County Hall, but this is simply because — like most Principals — he does not have responsibility for the overall situation. He cannot see the wood for the trees. The two Governors are pretty representative of their breed — what more can one say? So far as the task of interviewing is concerned, the DEO has had his fair share. When he thinks about it, which is seldom, he feels that experience in the game is the sole criterion for success. The DEO's immediate problem is the timing of the interview board, which is destined to take place on a Friday. Bitter experience has shown that these blessed things tend to drag on, and this will mean that, once again, he will arrive home late — another weekend off to a bad start.

So — when this particular board convenes, the interviewing environment will contain from the outset a number of pollutants:

1   A severe personality clash between Governor A and Governor B.
2   Considerable bias on the part of Governor A, of a wildly subjective and emotive nature.
3   A determination on the part of Governor B to be the star of the proceedings — any proceedings.
4   A bias on the Principal's part against bureaucratic interference from County Hall, exemplified in the person of the DEO — whom he regards as professionally incompetent in the role of selector.
5   An awareness by the Principal, rightly or wrongly, of the political implications of the proceedings.
6   A serious pre-judgement of the selection issue by the Principal and an attempt by him to influence others — downright selection skulduggery.
7   A *laissez-faire* attitude on the part of the DEO and a quite unforgiveable determination to push the proceedings along, simply to get home on time.

This is not a picture painted larger than life. The illustration provided is a very typical example of the attitudes and interactions that can, and do, influence the working and eventual outcome of far too many interview boards. There is but one comment to be made – Lord help the candidates. Also note, prith'ee, that a fair proportion of board worthies spend the entire proceedings trying to think up questions that will suitably impress the chairman, rather than encourage the candidate to come up with useful information. (*'Tell me, Mr Bloggs, what would be your reaction if such-and-such crisis occurred . . . ?'* and so on.)

There can only be a part-solution to the vexed problem of interview boards. Members should be chosen with infinite care – for the purposes of selection, not decoration – and everyone should be fully aware that *employment interviewing is a deadly serious business.* They should not lose sight of the fact that, in acting out their ego-tripping roles, they are playing with people's lives *and* the future well-being of the organisation they are privileged to represent. Bias, emotion, tradition and fantasy are not ingredients of the selection recipe – the rules of the game must be observed punctiliously and with utter disregard for personal feelings.

Now – back to more general, nitty-gritty topics ....

Opening gambits

The opening gambits of any employment interview must be directed towards the sole aim of placing the candidate at his ease. Then and only then will he give of his best. However, it is a sad fact of interviewing life that many interviewers find the task of relaxing a candidate very difficult to achieve. Innate shyness on the part of the interviewer often ensures that things get off to a stilted and worrying start. Some older interviewers – who lack extensive education and other formal qualifications – experience a sense of inferiority when faced with highly qualified applicants and, again, the session starts badly. Interviewers who display aggressive or overbearing attitudes – indicted more fully in Chapter 5 – will never attain the vital aim of a purposeful, steered and *pleasant* conversation.

Opening gambits are legion in extent and variety. Actions often speak louder than words, and the interviewer who rises from his deck and moves across the office to shake hands with the candidate has started to break the ice. The wise interviewer will always spend a couple of minutes discussing inconsequentials – and, unless a howling storm is raging at the time, he will manage to avoid mentioning the weather. Why not have a small selection of 'openers' up your interviewing sleeve?

How did you come here this morning ... ?
What were the roads like ... ?
Is that a good train service ... ?
Did you come via ... ?
What car do you run ...
That's interesting — do you ever get so-and-so trouble with it ... ?

Did you have any difficulty finding our office ... ?
Can you think of any improvements we could make ... ?

I see you come from so-and-so — what do you think of the area ... ?
and so on ...

A word on this question of innate shyness — do take heart, if you suffer from interview nerves, from the fact that the candidate will almost certainly be feeling worse than you. The opening gambit is intended to help *him* and, if you put your heart into the task of relaxing him, you will forget your own, lesser problem. *The candidate needs your help.* The interviewer who feels a sense of inferiority or inadequacy when facing a highly qualified candidate should always remember that *he is where he is because — formal qualifications or not — he has earned his position.* He may have left school at fourteen or what-have-you, with no GCEs, but he enjoys the tremendous advantage of accrued wisdom and hard experience — and that is why he is interviewing the candidate.

Interview plans

A very great deal has been written about interview plans and, for a reason which I shall explain later, I do not intend to engage in a welter of repetition. Suffice it to say that two widely known plans for assessing interview candidates are the *Five-fold Grading Scheme* propounded by Munro Fraser and the *Seven Point Plan* produced by Professor Roger.
   The *Five-fold Grading Scheme* covers:

1   *Impact on others*   Physical make-up, manner, appearance and speech.
2   *Qualifications*   Education and other attainments, experience.
3   *Innate abilities*   Qualities of comprehension and aptitude for learning.
4   *Motivation*   Quality of the goals set by the individual, his consistency and determination in following them up, his success in achieving them.
5   *Adjustment*   Emotional stability, ability to withstand stress, ability to get on with others.

The *Seven Point Plan* covers:

1 *Physical make-up*   Health, bearing, appearance, speech.
2 *Attainments*   Education, qualifications, experience.
3 *General intelligence*   Basic intellectual ability.
4 *Specific aptitudes*   Mechanical and manual dexterity, literacy and numeracy.
5 *Interests*   Intellectual, practical, physically active, artistic, social.
6 *Disposition*   Maturity, dependability, self-reliance, etc.
7 *Circumstances*   Domestic and other relevant circumstances.

These systems and many others are in widespread use by interviewers, but proper training is an essential prerequisite for success. It is for this reason that I am reluctant to deal in any great detail with such plans. I prefer to concentrate upon a more down-to-earth approach. It is for the reader to decide when and if he is ready to proceed to more sophisticated interviewing planning techniques. For the present, we are concerned with basics.

If an interviewer is to have anything engraved upon his heart, it should be the single, golden rule for interview planning – *start at the beginning and work through to the end.* In other words, decide the age point at which the background investigation is to commence and proceed, in near chronological order, through to the present day. The course of the interview will be liberally punctuated with side-issues, 'back-tracks' and umpteen points of interest – which will all result in the planned discussion sliding off on one tangent after the other. This will not matter, *provided that the conversation is steered back to the chronological mainstream of events in the candidate's history.* Here is a typical list of 'interview milestones' to cover most contingencies:

Initial phase questions for the interview with a young person

    Details of birth
    Family locations to present
    Family details
    Candidates' views/plans on marriage

Then

    First school – type, age of entry
    Transfer to next school – reasons, type, dates, activities

Other schools
Last school organisation — a possible starting point for
applicant with minimal history
Examinations
School sports
School clubs and societies
Youth organisations
Other hobbies and activities
Holiday activities/earning money
Career choice — action, plans
First job — how, reasons
Duties, responsibilities, progress
Plans, reasons for leaving
(Successive jobs in similar vein)
Current domestic/marital position
Spare-time activities/holidays
Plans and ambitions for the future

Quite plainly, a little thought should be given to the 'starting point'
of any background investigation. The middle-aged applicant will
not take kindly to a battery of questions about his schooling and,
in any event, such an investigation would serve little practical
purpose. Conversely, the young school-leaver — or the chap with
a minimal employment history — has only his childhood-cum-teenage
life to offer for examination, and this must be probed in some depth.
I well recall the rallying cry used by one lecturer who specialised in
interviewing techniques —

An achiever is an achiever is an achiever ....

Be it schooldays or many years in employment, *the past achievements
of candidates are the predictors of success or failure in the future.*

(see overleaf for self-tutorial)

Self-tutorial

A GENERAL QUIZ ON THE PRECEDING CHAPTER

Answers

Questions

1 Just to rub it in — what is the *real* purpose of the employment interview?

1 To carry out a comprehensive and accurate background investigation, to seek out and verify the facts of past achievement and failure.

2 Can group interviews be effective?

2 Yes — provided the members are selected with great care and, preferably, trained in interview techniques.

3 Why are opening gambits vital to the success of the interview?

3 They are the means by which the candidate is placed at ease. A relaxed candidate will give of his best.

4 What is the important rule for planning an investigation of a candidate's background?

4 Start at the beginning and work through to the end!

5 What, then, is it necessary to prepare before commencing an employment interview?

5 An interview plan — listing the 'milestones' of a typical history as an aide-memoire to effective questioning order.

6 What is the danger inherent in all planned interviews?

6 Well, in fact, there are many — but I have in mind the danger of being side-tracked and failing to return to the chronological 'mainstream'.

Nay, who but infants question in such wise?

Danté Gabriel Rossetti, 'Fragment'

5

ASKING THE RIGHT QUESTIONS IN THE RIGHT WAY

Open-ended questions

The crux of employment interviewing technique is that the interview is not, and should not appear to be, an interrogation. It must be conducted as a purposeful and steered conversation, with the aim of establishing conditions in which the candidate will reveal accurate and comprehensive factual information about himself. A further need is to control the interview in such a way as to ensure that irrelevancies are kept to a minimum and essential information emerges as quickly as possible. One valuable method by which these aims may be achieved is the use throughout the interview of *open-ended questions*. I will go further. Once an interviewer employs this form of questioning, he will find that his level of effort — in terms of actual speaking and mental planning — is drastically reduced. The candidate will have to supply positive and revealing answers and, in short, will be doing most of the work, whilst the interviewer considers and assesses the replies. What, then, are open-ended questions? Quite simply, questions asking:

WHAT   *What* were your duties...?
                What did you do then...?
                What subjects did you take...?
                What happened then...?
                What sort of...?

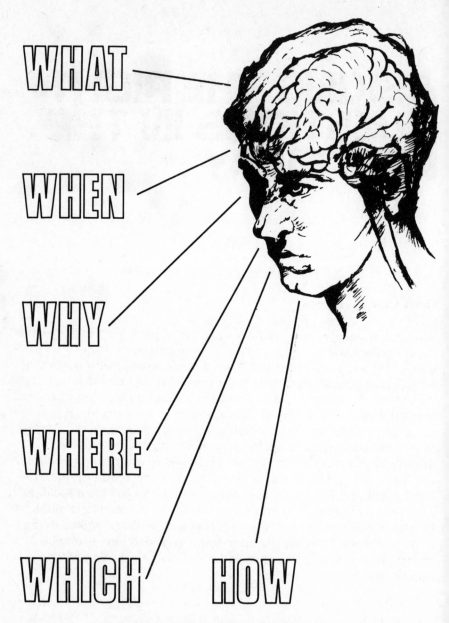

Figure 2   The key to open-ended questions

WHEN	*When* was that...?
	When did that happen...?
	When did you go...?
	When did you decide...?
	When did the company...?
WHY	*Why* was that...?
	Why did you choose...?
	Why do you think that...?
	Why did you do...?
	Why did they...?
WHERE	*Where* was that...?
	Where did you go next...?
	Where were you when...?
	Where did you do...?
	Where do you think...?
WHICH	*Which* school was that...?
	Which course did you...?
	Which were your best...?
	Which department was...?
	Which was that...?
HOW	*How* did that come about...?
	How do you think that...?
	How much did that...?
	How did you get...?
	How was that...?

The *manner* in which open-ended questions are asked will determine whether the interview is an interrogation or, as should be the case, a steered and friendly discussion. The interviewer should display a marked interest in the candidate and, although there is an overall need for the conversation to be firmly controlled by the interviewer, the candidate should feel that he is being treated with a degree of importance.

The interviewing jungle has many pitfalls for the inexperienced or naive interviewer and it is essential to remember some of the more common errors. Some are discussed in the following sections.

Direct questions

Direct questions are those that prompt a 'Yes' or 'No' answer:

> Did you take any examinations at school?
> Were you born in Cambridge?
> Do you have any hobbies?

It is virtually impossible to avoid asking some direct questions, but
every effort should be made to limit their use. An excessive number
of direct questions will guarantee that minimal information is
supplied by the candidate, and the unfortunate interviewer will
find that he has little or no time in which to think of the next
question — let alone plan the interview. The inevitable result will be
a mental flurry and the candidate will swiftly discern that something is wrong — to the further detriment of the interview in general.
There are some interviewers who persist in conducting an interview
by means of constant reference to the candidate's application form:

Ah, I see you sat the 'O' Level examinations?	(Yes)
Good — and passed in five subjects!	(Yes)
Did you find them very difficult?	(Er — fairly)
Well, it was a good result — then you left school?	(Yes)
Had you made up your mind about a career before leaving school?	(Not really)
But you decided to apply to — what's this firm? — Browns Limited?	(Yes)
And you became a junior clerk?	(Yes)
I see that you worked in the sales department?	(Er — yes)
Did you enjoy the work?	(Yes)
And, after this, you went to British Rail?	(That's right)
and so on....	

The above example has not been invented for the occasion — many
interviews are conducted in exactly this manner, with a positive
avalanche of direct questions producing nothing in the way of
fresh information.

Standard-revealing questions

Standard-revealing questions are those that tend to reveal the
personal beliefs or standards of the interviewer:

I'm an outdoor type — do you like outdoor activities?
An executive always works long hours — would you be prepared
   to work overtime?

Standard-revealing questions will always tempt the candidate to
respond in a manner calculated to impress the interviewer and agree
with his views — particularly if the questions are of a general nature.
Faced with replies which appear to fall in line with his own standards,
the naive interviewer may even be impressed — 'Jolly good chap this,
he has some sensible views...'.
   It sometimes happens within the paternalistic organisation that
interviewers are so imbued with the 'party line' that they make
regular and unconscious use of standard-revealing questions — but,
this time, questions that tend to reveal the standards of the
organisation, as opposed to the individual:

   We place great faith in our house magazine as a medium of
      communication — are you in favour of house journals?
   We at Brown Brothers believe wholeheartedly in evening
      courses — would you be willing to attend night-school?

The same comments apply; standard-revealing questions should be
avoided at all costs.

Insistence on showing authority

There is the odd interviewer who, rather than let the candidate
utter a word, will commence an interview by launching into an
impressive and long-winded exposition of his own prowess and
singular importance within the organisation:

   'I think that before we start, you should hear something about
   this company.... I formed it twenty-five years ago, absolutely
   from scratch, and all that you see here today is the result of
   my hard work over the years — pretty good, eh? All my team
   know that the entire operation rests on my shoulders, that I
   am the boss and what I say goes....'

Not possible? Larger than life? I know of one self-made employer
who invariably commences an interview in this fashion; needless to
say, he is not a very popular boss and he does seem to suffer a
fairly hefty rate of labour turnover.
   There are also those interviewers who, quite unconsciously,
adopt an 'interview manner' just before the candidate enters the

room — shoulders back, hands on desk, stern expression, clipped voice; the very epitome of authority. This may be fine for the disciplinary interview but it is quite wrong and potentially damaging so far as the employment interview is concerned.

Aggression

A mighty hard pill for many interviewers to swallow is the simple fact that, whatever the temptation, they must display the patience of Job. There are always 'difficult' candidates who, by dint of abrasive and irritating personalities, mannerisms and what-have-you, will tend to aggravate and annoy the interviewer. The temptation to take such candidates down a peg or two must be resisted — for aggression, in any shape or form, is inexcusable. Remember that the interview, effectively controlled by the imposition of a firm and friendly authority, is a tool of selection and candidates must be given full rein to display their good *and* bad attributes. Another fact of interviewing life is that it is totally wrong for the interviewer to employ a style of questioning that would be better suited to the barrack square, for this is merely another form of aggression — beware, then, the liverish feeling and the desire to kick out.

Argument

There are some of us who cannot pass the time of day without engaging in argument, and there are certainly some interviewers who cannot allow a single response by the candidate to pass unchallenged. There is a world of difference between discussion and argument, and it is grossly unfair to place an interview candidate — already labouring under the disadvantage of being in the proverbial hot-seat — at further disadvantage. All of which brings me to the vexed question of stress interviews....

Stress interviewing, a popular gambit in the selection of salesmen and insurance representatives, is a technique developed to assess whether candidates can resist pressure — and the use of argument figures largely in the process. There is little doubt that stress interviews, expertly conducted by qualified and experienced interviewers, reveal characteristics which appear only infrequently in candidates' normal activities and behaviour — *but the technique needs to be used with great caution and only by trained administrators.*

Domination

Extroverts — effervescent characters, voluble speakers, arm-wavers — we have all encountered these very energetic people and a lot of them carry out employment interviews. The interview which is dominated by that fearsome beast, the 'thrusting executive', who pins the candidate to his seat by sheer force of personality, is a pretty chilling affair. Strangely enough, many such interviewers have immense difficulty in carrying out their post-interview appraisals, presumably because they have been carried away by their own self-ebullience during the session. Be that as it may, the employment interview represents a time of stress for any candidate who really wants the job concerned and is aware that he is competing against others, and no factor should be allowed to add to that stress. It should be remembered that very many first-class employees do not, and cannot, perform well at interview long after they have joined the company — let alone beforehand. Domination by the interviewer can only inhibit the candidate and mar the selection process.

Giving advice and moralising

I once witnessed an interview of a young person by a very kindly and 'caring' employer. Everything started well; the candidate was made to feel at ease, the questions were virtually all open-ended, the interviewer was achieving his objective — until, suddenly, the entire session went to pieces. In reply to a question about his parents, the candidate revealed that his mother suffered from severe osteo-arthritis; whereupon, instead of making a short comment in sympathy, the kindly man proceeded to interview the youngster on the subject of his mother's ailment. Questions about her treatment, advice and suggestions concerning probable courses of action — it went on and on.... The point is simply this; an employment interview must never become the vehicle for a counselling session, the interviewer must not allow himself to be side-tracked into giving advice or moralising, for this serves no purpose in the selection process.

Losing control

As I have already stated, not all candidates will be respectful, moderate, 'nice to know' people. A few, hopefully a very few, will be the direct opposite; individuals who will have the interviewer gnashing his teeth and hanging on to urbanity by a thread of self-control —

57

and hang on he must. Whatever the provocation, however bad the circumstances, *the interviewer must never, ever lose control of himself.* If things have progressed way beyond redemption, the interview must be terminated, politely and quickly; if not, the situation must be remedied with carefully chosen and effective comment.

There is, of course, another form of 'losing control' – losing control of the interview. Not all of us are born to paint and – since interviewing is also an art – not all of us will ever be proficient interviewers. To such people, the employment interview will be an ordeal, anticipated with dread and conducted under very real stress. Unfortunately, the interviewer's state of mind will communicate itself to the candidate, who may succeed in 'taking over' the interview. The candidate will tend to dominate the proceedings and may ask the bulk of the questions – the interviewer becomes the interviewee. Loss of control has taken place and the session is no longer a valid selection process. So – perceptive bosses, mark well; such interviews must not be permitted to take place. It is little short of cruelty and most certainly unproductive to require totally unsuited members of staff to conduct employment interviews. Note, also, that formal training will probably be of little avail in correcting the situation; the innately shy person is best employed away from the interviewing scene.

Self-tutorial

AN EXERCISE ON INTERVIEW QUESTIONS

Recalling some of the common errors in questioning technique, there follows an exercise in which you are invited to examine the questions and spot the errors involved. You should test yourself by suggesting a better alternative in each case.

1   Did you come here by train?

2   Were you born in Oxford?

3   Did you do well at school?

4   You say that you did fairly well at geography, but I don't think that an examination mark of 51 per cent really bears this out – do you?

5   I see that you arrived ten minutes late for this interview – I hope that there's a good reason for this. Why were you late?

6   Do you appreciate that, as Personnel Manager, I am totally responsible for maintaining the company workforce?

7   Gliding is a complete mystery to me — tell me about it.

8   The successful applicant for this post will be required to control the staff with a firm hand — would you be capable of this?

9   Do you have any hobbies?

10   I've studied your application very closely and, whilst I think it's a pretty good piece of work, I do suggest that you type any future applications. This makes them much easier to read and, you never know, might impress whoever receives them! Ah, yes, and I do suggest that you try to list more hobbies and interests — people like to see them, you know.

11   Presumably you are ambitious?

12   In your last job, were you responsible for cash transactions, or was that your assistant's responsibility, and what was the system for balancing and checking the cash account?

13   Do you have strong political views?

14   If a bomb exploded in this building right now, what would you do?

Well — How did you do?

Here are some guideline answers:

Question 1   A *direct question* and useless. The question *'How did you come here?'* is a useful settling-in gambit at the commencement of an interview.

Question 2   Again, a *direct question* and useless — *'Where* were you born?'

Question 3   Another *direct question* which also tends to be *standard-revealing.* It is also far too vague for use in investigating progress at school.

Question 4   *Argumentative* and *standard-revealing* — the type of question to be avoided. The question *'How* do *you* rate your geography examination result?'* might be of some value.

Question 5 Having heard the reason for the candidate's late arrival, what will the interviewer do — place him on a charge? This is a nasty example of *aggression*.

Question 6 *Insistence on showing authority* and a *direct question* to boot. Perhaps the poor candidate is expected to stand up and bow three times in deference to this exalted interviewer . . . .

Question 7 No — this is a *standard-revealing* question, this time of ignorance. Refer to my comments in Chapter 6; *never* betray an ignorance in this manner, it is not necessary.

Question 8 Again, *standard-revealing* — the candidate would have to be an idiot or a saint to answer other than 'yes' — it's also another *direct question*.

Question 9 A simple *direct question* — the interviewer may be fortunate in that the candidate will say 'yes' and go on to describe his hobbies, but far better to ask, '*What* do you do in your spare time?'

Question 10 An example of *giving advice,* which has no place in the employment interview. Note, also, the time which is wasted . . . .

Question 11 *Direct, standard-revealing* and a waste of time.

Question 12 A terrible hotch-potch and *far too long* — three questions in one, with at least one *direct question*. Ask one question at a time.

Question 13 Yuk! A *direct question* and — unless asked in the context of an interview for a political agent's job — forbidden.

Question 14 A *nonsense question* — a typical Colonel Blimp-like gambit. Some interviewers have a penchant for these way-out questions in the belief that they will be able to detect aspects of a candidate's personality from the manner in which he replies. Not so in most cases — the interviewer will be revealing his personality to the candidate.

Take heart — when the crunch comes, you will still pose direct questions but, hopefully, they will be few in number. This is a game in which practice makes perfect and, for good practice, why not try that old radio game in which questions are asked, and the first person to give a 'yes' or 'no' answer loses a point? The questioner will soon appreciate the doubtful value of direct questions.

*The true use of speech is not so much to express
our wants as to conceal them.*

Goldsmith, 'The Use of Language'

6

ROGUES, CHEATS AND VAGABONDS

Securing a job — the right job — is often a marathon task. The stress involved in locating a suitable vacancy can be formidable, particularly when the job-seeker is dogged by unemployment, but there is worse to follow. Having found a likely opening, the applicant has then to secure an interview — a daunting prospect of competition against heavy odds which, more often than not, will include the traditional hurdle of 'short-listing'. The issue is plain; whatever his skills, the applicant must assume the role of author-cum-editor and produce a written case which, presenting the right facts in exactly the right style, will appeal to the totally unknown prospective employer. Little wonder that much time is spent in completing impressive personal histories and that many applicants resort to a degree of embroidery when compiling these documents. Unfortunately for the interviewer, there are also candidates who will not hesitate to engage in downright skulduggery when completing their applications. Facts will be distorted and pure invention becomes the name of the application game. Quite obviously, such exaggerations and deliberate falsehoods will be maintained at the interview stage and, even in the face of quite astute questioning, many rogue candidates will succeed in convincing the interviewer that all is well and above board. Let me stress once again that *the purpose of the employment interview is to carry out a comprehensive and accurate background investigation — the interviewer must seek out and verify facts.* The object of this chapter is to highlight some of the tricks of the interviewing trade which, put to discerning use, will enable the proficient interviewer to separate fact from fiction.

63

The candidate with a yen for embroidery

There are two topic areas within a personal history account which positively invite exaggeration — the description of employment responsibilities and the listing of hobbies and interests. Interviewer, mark them well.

Employment responsibilities

Take, for example, the applicant who, previously employed in the buying department of a company, completes this section with the words, *'Responsible for all contracts'*. The unwary interviewer may well ask general questions which enable the candidate to display a good working knowledge of contract administration; sufficient, in fact, to apparently confirm the statement on the application. However, the truth may well be that the applicant, whilst familiar with the overall work of the department, was only responsible for the *safe custody* of all contracts — a vastly different kettle of fish. The proficient interviewer will probe such statements by first questioning the candidate about the responsibilities of the senior people in the department, thereby limiting the applicant to a more accurate expression of his own personal responsibilities.

Since it is fairly common practice to authenticate an applicant's current or last job by means of a reference (of which more anon), it is likely that exaggerated employment responsibilities will be confined to earlier job histories — the candidate with a yen for embroidery is seldom a fool.

Hobbies and interests

Most application forms and personal histories refer to hobbies and spare-time interests, for this information — when linked with the employment history — will present a full spectrum of past achievement. However, the topic also provides an ideal opportunity for many applicants to embroider facts and inject a little sparkle into an otherwise mundane self-portrait. The poor interviewer, faced with the need to sort out the wheat from the chaff, will often be faced with impressive hobbies and interests of which he has scant personal knowledge — how can he arrive at the truth?

Picture, if you will, the applicant who spends most of his leisure time glued to the television — the Walter Mitty of a press-button technology. Faced with the need to list spare-time pursuits, he feels that he must present a desirable image and, looking back over months of devotion to the goggle-box, he experiences some concern. Then, remembering that late-night showing of *The Guns of Navarone*, inspiration strikes — *Mountaineering* will do for a start .... A little more memory-prodding and a recollection of that gorgeous Bionic Woman — lo and behold, *Parachuting* joins the list. Our hero then seeks to leaven the mix with a touch of normality and swiftly adds, *Reading*. Task completed; it's a safe bet that the interviewer will be duly impressed and almost certainly ill-qualified to question either of the two main choices. The sad fact is that, unless the interviewer uses a little cunning, he will fail to arrive at the truth; so — be cunning. If the proficient interviewer wishes to probe this candidate's prowess in mountaineering, he will pose the type of question which requires little knowledge of the subject and, more to the point, will place the applicant well and truly on the proverbial hot-seat:

> *'Tell me, if you were required to advise a young man who wished to take up mountaineering, what equipment would you advise him to buy?'*

> *'How should he make a start in this hobby?'*

The candidate, required to do all the work, will swiftly reveal the true extent of his knowledge of the subject and will enable the interviewer to form a quite accurate assessment of the subject's *actual* participation and level of interest.

The practical interviewer, if not the moralist, will recognise that there is a world of difference between the applicant who tends to over-indulge his window-dressing and the utter rogue; the former usually embroiders because he has a vacuum to hide, the latter invariably lies *because he has something very real to hide.* If there is a Hades for people in the selection game, it is probably lined with interviewers who have claimed, 'I know a liar when I see one ... '. Unable, I would hope, to resort to police methods of interrogation, which have no place in the employment interview, the interviewer must use all the skills at his command to detect the liar. This is no mean task.

The candidate with something to hide

First, let us examine the obvious areas in which an applicant is most likely to conceal the truth by lying in his teeth; past employment, qualifications and experience spring to mind.

Lies which relate to past employment

Motives for such falsehoods will include:

1   Concealment of a dismissal for misconduct or incompetency by substituting a plausible account of resignation or redundancy.
2   Total misrepresentation of a job function in order to obtain a better but undeserved post.
3   Total invention of a particular job in order to conceal a period of unemployment or, worse, imprisonment.
4   In the case of a congenital liar, complete distortion and invention stemming from psychological disturbance.

Lies which relate to qualifications and experience

These falsehoods are usually concerned with requirements spelt out in the job advertisement or specification but which, in the opinion of the applicant, are only indirectly connected with the actual job function. Thus, an applicant for a personnel manager appointment which carries a requirement of membership of the Institute of Personnel Management may, if he lacks this qualification, lay false claim to being an MIPM — he is confident that his experience and knowledge will carry him through. Again, many candidates who resort to false claims of past experience will do so in the blithe conviction that a general knowledge of the work concerned will enable them to perform the new job satisfactorily — 'picking the rest up as they go along'.
   Once the interviewer is familiar with the more obvious areas in which lies may be encountered, he can resort to the simple but totally effective expedient of making the necessary telephone calls — before the interview takes place. In my experience, very few interviewers carry out this obvious and straightforward check, which really should be written into the standard operating procedure of any employment interviewing policy. It should be noted that I advocate the telephone in preference to the letter; not only is it quicker, but people will be far more frank when they are not required to commit their remarks to paper. With regard to formal qualifications, I am continually astonished at the number of otherwise efficient executives who, having specified various qualifications as vital to the advertised post, then fail to ask for documentary evidence at the interview. Let us suppose, however, that documents *are* produced — is this sufficient? Take, for instance, the certificate of membership issued five years ago — kept carefully by the candidate, notwithstanding that his subscription lapsed two

years ago; the document is quite worthless. A quick tip for use in these inflationary times; if membership has lapsed, the candidate may not be aware of the current subscription rate — but, naturally, the interviewer will have checked! An odd question or two about the activities of the body concerned will often reveal a surprising ignorance on the part of the candidate — why not try?

Having already implied in this chapter that the discovery of liars by simply observing people is a practice strictly for the birds, it is nevertheless vital to watch the candidate closely during an interview. This does not mean that the poor unfortunate should be transfixed by a basilisk glare throughout the entire session but, rather, that the interviewer should watch for any tell-tale signs that might occur. A sudden blush, hesitation or change in demeanour may — just may — give the game away, but I would counsel extreme caution when interpreting such phenomena! It is not within my terms of reference to pronounce on the cause, effect or efficacy of such 'in things' as the proclaimed science of body-language, or the esoteric art of learning a candidate's innermost secrets by tracking his eyeballs — suffice it to say that keen observation may pay dividends.

The vexed question of references

References — an area in which we all cheat. Almost every candidate for a job is required to furnish referees — one associated with his current or last employment and one or two others who will supply 'evidence of character'. The rules of this great British game vary from place to place; sometimes, the successful candidate is actually permitted to commence his new job 'subject to the receipt of satisfactory references' or, as is more usually the case, the candidate's appointment is held over, pending receipt of the august documents. Why do we perpetuate this rank absurdity? How many *bad* references are written today? A candidate may have little choice when required to nominate his latest employer but, at worst, the result will only be non-committal — and, as for character referees, who would be fool enough to nominate an unreliable source?

The plain truth is that the vast majority of references are not worth the paper on which they are written. If an ex-employer's views on a candidate are required, they should be obtained by *telephone* — with gratifying results. It is true that some organisations do not permit references to be supplied over the telephone — pedants and arrant traditionalists remain in good supply — but, at least, the effort should be made. Character referees are best forgotten ....

False documents

Yes — false documents. The widespread availability of high-quality
copying machines has made it possible for even the most arrant
amateur to produce thoroughly convincing facsimiles of qualification
certificates and so on. Very few selectors tend to question the
production of photostat copies of such papers, but they should
Consider, for instance, the young applicant with a very sparse
education certificate; given a little imagination and a lot of dishonesty,
he merely has to follow the recipe:

> Take one document and using one of the excellent proprietary
> brands available, 'white out' all typewritten entries. Substitute
> in the appropriate spaces the desired entries, preferably using
> a typewriter with a carbon ribbon. Photostat — observing that
> the white blobs do not appear on the copy — and serve ....

A word on degrees. How many interviewers in the business world
have actually *seen* a degree parchment? Many advertisements for
executive and technical appointments require a degree qualification
but, incredibly, many of the interviewers who are actually involved
in selection for these jobs have little or no knowledge of the
documents concerned. There have been some resounding cases of
clever but crooked applicants submitting gloriously inscribed parch-
ments in Latin — imposing but completely false. Remember that a
home printing press is just not necessary; some basic artistic talent,
the right paper and instant lettering — glazed with the special
aerosol spray varnish sold for the purpose — and near-perfect
documents are entirely possible.

Variations on the theme of false documents are infinite. There is
even the example of a perfectly genuine technical certificate, used
by the young man who actually won it in fair competition — but
used it in completely false circumstances.... The young man in question
applied for a job as a motor vehicle mechanic, and produced his
technical course certificate as evidence of his qualification for the
job. At the interview, the youngster explained that he had taken the
course at the local technical college and, since the vital certificate
was there for inspection, the interviewer had absolutely no reason
to doubt the lad's word. It was a few months after the lad had
started work that, quite by chance, it was discovered that the
period of training had been spent, not at a technical college, but at
a Borstal. The course had taken place and the certificate had been
won — but 'within those walls!'

A note on concealed unemployment

Many applicants will be anxious to conceal the fact that they have been unemployed for a period, either for reasons of enforced redundancy or, more sinister, because they have been involuntary guests of Her Majesty. In the former case, there is little doubt that prolonged redundancy does not impress prospective employers — the taint of 'dead-wood' tends to stick, however unfairly — and many of the courses held for redundant executives actually recommend that redundancy should be concealed (by substituting sabbatical leave, etc). So far as ex-prisoners are concerned, the genuinely penitent and rehabilitated applicant knows full well the extent of his task in starting afresh. Since this book is concerned only with the techniques of employment interviewing, it is not for me to pronounce on the attitudes which should be adopted in such cases — except, perhaps, to remind the reader of the salutary provisions of *The Rehabilitation of Offenders Act, 1974.* Suffice it to say, for the umpteenth time, that the interviewer is merely interested in assimilating facts that will enable him to make a near-objective decision. Accepting this premise, the truth must be sought out and the interviewer should pay great attention to periods in a career history which could be other than that which the candidate has claimed. Statements by applicants that they deliberately brought their employment to a close in order to research some technique or other, or pursue a course of home study, should not be accepted without complete validation.

Self-tutorial

ARRIVING AT THE TRUTH

The following 'mini-scripts' are not offered as texts which should be learned by heart — they are merely examples of *open-ended questions*, arranged in a logical sequence, which, if followed as a guide, *will enable the interviewer to arrive at the truth of a situation:*

Probing a candidate's job responsibilities

What did you do then?

How did this come about?

How many staff were there in this department?

How was the department organised?

To *whom* were you directly responsible?

What were his duties?

Fine — now, *what* were your duties?

How many staff worked directly for you?

Briefly — *what* were their duties?

What was your commencing salary at this job?

When you took this job, *what* were your plans and ambitions for the future?

How did things work out?

Why did you leave?

What was your salary when you left?

What did you do then?

Probing hobbies and interests

Let's get away from work — *what* sports do you play?

Which are you best at?

Which team are you in?

How often do you play?

Who runs the team?

What other games did you say you play?

Leaving sports then — *what* clubs and societies are available in your area?

Which interest you?

What part do you play in the Judo Club?

What does that involve?

How long does that take you?

What do you have to do?

Apart from all this — *what* else do you do in your spare time?

How did this come about?

How many models have you made?

Why do you specialise in this way?

How do you keep up-to-date in the modelling world?

What is your most successful model?

How would you advise a beginner in this hobby?

You mentioned reading — *what* sort of reading interests you?

Why is this?

What are you reading at the moment?

Who is your favourite author?

Why is that?

What other activities are you involved in just now?

Probing references

Thank you for supplying us with details of your referees — with regard to the first one, *what* is his position within the company?

What was your relationship with him?

How long has he been with the company?

When may we contact him?

Now — *why* have you nominated Mr Brown a referee of character?

What relationship is there between you?

What does Mr Brown do for a living?

When may we contact him?

Probing a period of 'study leave'

What influenced your decision to leave this job?

Why was that?

What made you decide to study personnel management?

How did that come about?

Where did you commence your studies?

What course was this?

Where was this?

How often were you required to attend there?

Who was your course tutor?

How long was the course?

What examinations did you take?

What were your results?

You seem to have coped very well — *how* did you manage financially during this period?

What about unemployment benefit?

What is the address of the college?

Fine — *how* has this study affected your plans and ambitions for the future?

Suggested tactics when dealing with dishonesty

Actual or suspected dishonesty on a candidate's part will normally mean rejection, and the interview is best terminated:

> Mr White — we have now arrived at the stage when I must give your case some very serious consideration. I therefore intend to leave things as they are for the time being *(stand up)* and I will be writing to you during the course of the next few days. Thank you for coming along this morning — I found our discussion of great interest — good morning to you . . . .

Note that no mention has been made of dishonesty — this would be a most unwise tactic. The follow-up letter should also refrain from mentioning the matter and, ideally, will merely follow the pattern of the normal, pleasant letter of rejection currently in use.

And differing judgements serve but to declare,
That truth lies somewhere, if we knew but where.

Cowper, 'Hope'

7

ASSESSING
THE CANDIDATE

'I'm sure that I don't use the right techniques when I interview applicants — but, for all that, I've always been fairly happy with the results. My personal troubles start when an interview is over — when I've got to come to some sort of a conclusion about the guy I've interviewed. Are you going to deal with this aspect on the course? I hope so, because I'm sure this is where I tend to come unstuck. I make a lot of notes after each interview — pretty soon after, in fact, because I've got a rotten memory. Then — when it comes to the crunch and I have to decide who gets a particular job, I find I'm back to square one.... I suppose there isn't really a foolproof method of picking out the best applicant, is there?'

'... when you've been in the game long enough, you get a feeling about the right one for the job....'

'Surely, after interviewing a number of people, it's the one that sticks uppermost in your mind that counts....'

'To be honest — and I hope this doesn't offend anyone — I think there's too much rubbish bandied about concerning this summing-up, or whatever it's called, to see who gets the job. Don't you agree...?'

(Comments made by delegates during the 'ice-breaker' session at the beginning of an interviewing course.)

If I am to be frank, I am continually surprised at the number of managers who, when asked to make general comment on the assessment of candidates after interview, tend to respond in vague or scathing terms. Somewhat emotional references are often made to 'back-room boys who pontificate from ivory towers' and the mumbo-jumbo of money-grubbing pseudo-management experts — barbed observations, aimed with accuracy and intent. Well, speaking from the long-lease tenancy of my ivory tower — but not, I trust, in mumbo-jumbo — I have one immediate pontification to offer. I very much doubt if these self-same managers would dream of making an important financial decision without first weighing all the relevant facts. Employee recruitment is about people and people tend to come expensive. They also have a habit of leaving in expensive style — remember Uncle TULRA, the Big Bad Wolf of errant employers.

Weighing the facts

One of the major questions to be considered is how much weight should be given to the facts about applicants. For example, some organisations — a very few — utilise various forms of ability testing as an objective adjunct to their interviewing procedures. In such cases, should test scores be given priority over interview judgements? The desirable procedure is for each organisation to determine what information has high predictive value and to decide how this information can be obtained most effectively. If interviewing is to be the only means of obtaining information, it must plainly concentrate on the verification of historical data — this has predictive value. It is then for the selector to weigh relevant facts against the detailed requirements of the job specification and to decide which candidate is best suited to the post. Easily said!

The rub comes when the interviewer makes written or — dire sin — mental notes on salient aspects of each candidate's verified history. At the end of the day, when he tries to compare notes and arrive at the big decision — what does he find? More often than not, it boils down to a motley collection of jottings or, in the case of the chap who relied on memory, a mental vacuum. Written notes *must* be made — but how best to make them? The short, sharp answer is that notes must be in a standardised format; some type of printed form is necessary.

I think I can guess the likely reaction of readers at this point. When lecturing on the subject and the time comes to drop the pearl about a printed assessment form being necessary, one can see a positive shudder run through the audience. So, without further preamble,

THIS SECTION IS FOR OFFICE USE ONLY

References requested ———— Call-Up letter sent ———

Interview Result SUCCESSFUL/UNSUCCESSFUL

Unsuccessful Notification Sent ———

Figure 3 A horrendous non-starter example of an interview assessment panel

Specification	Candidate Sue Harrison
EDUCATION Minimum GCE 'O' Eng Lang Mathematics	R.S.A. English + Maths (Grades II + I)
TRNG QUALIFICATIONS Tech Coll Sec Course - pass Typing/S'hand	Typing 30 w.p.m Shorthand 80 w.p.m
EXPERIENCE Prev emp as Clerk/Typist etc desirable	Worked at weekend (general dohs) for 6 mths - no real experience.
SPECIAL REQUIREMENTS Will be emp on receptionist duties following trng: pleasant manner	Seems O.K - polite, good looking girl.
DRIVING LICENCE required	No.

Figure 4 An attempt to provide a means of comparing job requirements with a candidate's attributes

let me say that I know how much you hate paperwork. I know that each and every training wallah advocates more and more bumph — and I know intimately the myriad arguments which boil down to time being your enemy. As a man who has managed at the sharp end for a number of years, I know there is good reason for such a reaction — but I must still advocate the use of this particular piece of paper. It is necessary and it works — I promise.

The interview assessment form — call it what you will — can only be effective if it gives positive help to the interviewer in composing his notes and provides him with a simple method of making comparisions between candidates. Unfortunately, many existing assessment forms fail to meet these fairly obvious criteria. This can best be illustrated by examining a small sample of such forms.

We commence with the ridiculous — see Figure 3. This panel, situated at the foot of a totally unsuitable application form (and therefore seen by all candidates), is a typical product of a bad administration. Believe it or not, the application form is used for

the selection and recruitment of professionally qualified people —
one wonders what applicants must think of the organisation
concerned. For the purposes of selection, it is pure rubbish.

In the example shown in Figure 4 a serious attempt has been
made to provide the interviewer with a means of comparing aspects
of the job specification with verified information on a candidate.
Whilst the form, of which only a section is illustrated, will enable
standardised notes to be made, it provides no means of comparison
between individual candidates. The interviewer is left to ferret

Prospect for _____				
	A	**B**	**C**	**D**
First impressions				
Appearance				
Speech				
Communication skill				
Education				
Training				
Experience				
Interests				
Initiative				
Leadership				
Motivation				
Attitudes				

Figure 5   A typical attempt at a graphic scale assessment panel

among his notes and, hopefully, find the words which will enable him to make a selection decision.

Figure 5 is a serious but misguided attempt to provide the interviewer with a means of assessing — rating — a candidate.

Current practice in assessment

Before proposing a type of interview assessment form which would be better suited to the selection task than those illustrated in Figures 3-5, it is necessary to take a look at current practice in the field of assessment or appraisal. Briefly, an appraisal system provides a rating form that is designed to highlight certain characteristics of an individual and, by various methods, to offer a means by which the assessments of several individuals can be compared.

The graphic scale method of assessment

The assessment form illustrated in Figure 5 is an attempt at a graphic scale, the most commonly used method. Graphic scales provide a list of the items to be appraised and a range of degrees for each item:

ITEM TO BE ASSESSED   *High Average Low*

Formal qualifications for the job   6 5 4 3 2 1

Letter grades may be used instead of numbers:

ITEM TO BE ASSESSED   *High Average Low*

Formal qualifications for the job   A B C D E F

In order to provide further help for the assessor, the rating scales are sometimes supplemented by 'triggers' — simple words or phrases such as *High, Average* and *Low* in the above examples. In addition to being required to mark the selected grade for each item, assessors may be required to justify their ratings with brief narrative observations.

Ranking systems

Ranking systems are probably the simplest methods of assessment, and merely require the assessor to rank individuals in order on each

RANKING SYSTEM

AMBITION		LEADERSHIP	
1	CLARKE	**1**	CLARKE
2	DREW	**2**	WHITE
3	JONES	**3**	JONES
4	SMITH	**4**	DREW
5	COOPER	**5**	SMITH
6	WHITE	**6**	COOPER

Figure 6   Part of a typical ranking system of assessment

prescribed item. A typical example of part of a ranking system is illustrated in Figure 6. Obviously, the system is only suitable for assessing small groups, but could lend itself to the short-list interviewing situation.

Checklist scales

Checklist scales are intended to reduce the assessors' work to a minimum and, for this reason, have been described — somewhat unkindly — as 'idiot boxes'. All the assessor is required to do is check with ticks the phrases which most closely describe the characteristics of the individual concerned. An example — which I cannot in all conscience recommend for use — is provided in Figure 7!

Errors to be avoided

In Chapter 1, I described the errors which can be committed by unwary interviewers. There is an almost indentical list of sins which

	5	4	3	2	1
PERSONAL HYGIENE	Was born vacuum-packed and has stayed thus	Emerges from water to feed	Washes regularly on every second Bank Holiday	Has proved that skin dissolves in water	Looks like a skunk – certainly smells like one
ORAL ABILITY	Verbal diarrhoea, vaccinated with a gramophone needle	Seen lecturing to herds of pedigree cattle	Occasionally talks in his sleep	Heard to grunt when he is trodden on	Burps when fed
LEADERSHIP	Invented the words "Carry on, sergeant"	Likes to see old ladies set an example by crossing roads on their own	Often picks up old ladies who happen to get knocked over	Sets an example by knocking them over himself	Never attempts to lead horses to water because he is never thirsty
VERBAL ABILITY	Never uses words of less than 63 letters & always in Sanskrit	Refers to G.B.S. as "My dear old Dad"	Published many works – all on lavatory walls	Can sign name when he can remember it	So who needs writing, anyway?

Figure 7   A checklist scale – certainly not typical and not recommended for use!

apply to assessment. One must bear in mind our human fallibilities and accept them as an ever-present risk:

The Error of Leniency   There is a tendency on the part of many assessors to exercise leniency — they cannot bring themselves to be (their words) 'too hard'. Well — yer pays yer money, yer takes yer choice.

The Error of Central Tendency   Some assessors are disinclined to make extreme judgements and restrict themselves to the central bands of rating scales. One way round this problem is to rate one item at a time for all the individuals — but, for obvious reasons, this should not be attempted when assessing interview candidates.

The Halo Error   An assessor tends to judge an individual in terms of a general mental attitude towards the individual's personality as a whole. Thus, the tendency is to over-rate the candidate whose personality is found pleasing. It must be appreciated that an individual can be 'excellent' in one quality and 'poor' in another — and almost certainly is.

The Logical Error   Assessors are inclined to award similar ratings in respect of items that *seem* logically related, i.e. the quick thinker may not be intelligent.

The Contrast Error   With this error, there is a tendency for the assessor to rate others in the opposite direction from himself in a given characteristic. Self-preservation — it happens and must not.

The Proximity Error   Neighbouring items on an assessment form tend to be rated similarly — no real thought is being given to a valid assessment of each and every characteristic.

A suggested approach

The first task in designing an interview assessment form is to compile a valid and comprehensive list of the items to be measured. Bearing in mind that the interviewer is primarily concerned with the question of historical data, the items should be restricted — as far as is possible and unlike the example in Figure 7 — to factual elements. Characteristics such as reliability, initiative, etc., lend themselves to wildly subjective interpretation — use them with care.

A suggested approach is illustrated in Figure 8. Note that Part

JOB SPECIFICATION

FOR _MANAGEMENT ACCOUNTANT_

Responsible to Ch. Acct'nt. £2,900
(pt. ICMA), c. £4,500 (qual. ICMA)
Company car – Pension scheme – BUPA
on comp. 2 yrs.

						Poor	Fair	Average –	Average +	Very Good	Superlative
						F	**E**	**D**	**C**	**B**	**A**
Education Quals.	Univ. standard									X	
Prof. Exam. Quals.	BA(Hons) Bus Studies Ideally ICMA or part thereof									X	
Non-Exam. Quals.											
Relevant Exp'nce	18 mths exp in ind. & 1 yr sandwich course exp.								X		
Physical Quals.										X	
S/time Interests	Ideally evidence of pers initiative and exp in organising							X			
Oral Expression	Ability to communicate with sen. management essential							X			
Appearance	Executive status								X		

Notes   Full driving licence reqd.

Post involves mobility throughout UK.
Successful applicant must undertake to
complete ICMA if not already qualified.

Notes Driving Licence O.K.
Taking ICMA Finals 1978
(1st Class Honours BA)
22 months in Cost acctg + 1 yr
sandwich in general acctg.
Adequate speaker but some
shyness – should improve.

Figure 8   A suggested approach to interview assessment

A of the form contains the list of items to be assessed and that Part B, the assessment panel, is a separate piece of paper. Thus, Part A serves as a master list, capable of quick and easy matching with a separate part B for each candidate.

Part A   In the example, the form has been printed with the key items which will apply, in greater or lesser degree, to all professional and executive staff appointments. Provision has been made for these key items to be further defined in order to reflect the detailed requirements of a particular job specification.

Part B   The assessment panel in the example is a graphic scale, employing a letter grading from A to F with 'triggers' ('Average +', etc.) to further help the assessor. Note that the use of six grades precludes a 'middle-average' assessment — an additional spur to encourage thought on the part of the assessor. The paper is also provided with a space (and overleaf, of course) for narrative comment, which will be an essential chore once key points have been rated in a logical and standardised form.

So, there we have it — a bare-bones example of a suggested assessment form. But this is not all. Despite all my insistence throughout these pages on the primary need to seek out and assess factual data, there remain two burning questions which beset all interviewers:

> Does the candidate possess the right motivation — the fire in the belly — for the job?
> Will he fit in?

For the great majority of us, the answers are expressed in the 'gut-feeling' which assails our consciousness during the interview — a summation, or distillation, of all the impressions we have formed of the candidate as the session proceeds. This gut-feeling — a slightly vulgar but highly accurate and descriptive term — cannot be ignored. In fact, the sheer strength of its emotive influence on the interviewer's judgement is such that it constitutes a prime factor in the selection process. The validity of the questions cannot be open to doubt; the quality of a candidate's motivation and the consideration of whether he will 'fit in' are vital aspects which command attention. Unfortunately and for the umpteenth time, *homo sapiens* is singularly ill-equipped to come up with the right answer. How, then, can one make the best of a bad job? I think the only alternative — having formed the gut-feeling — is to subject ourselves to a series of questions which require completely frank answers:

Assessing motivation

1   Why is the candidate interested in the vacancy?
2   Why is he looking for another appointment?
3   What has he discovered about the organisation?
4   Why has he left previous jobs? Are any of the causes likely to recur in the new job?
5   Has he followed a definite career pattern to date and is he realising his aims?
6   Does the new job constitute a logical step in his career pattern?
7   Are his personal strengths consistent with the major demands of the new job?
8   Has he asked intelligent and searching questions about the new job, the conditions of employment and the organisation in general?

Will he fit in?

1   Are his manner, speech and attitudes suitable for the current vacancy, and will they be a credit to the organisation or department as a whole?
2   Are they natural, or were they assumed for the purposes of the selection process?
3   Will he be able to work in harmony with his new *colleagues* — and exclude yourself from this question!

Having deliberated as objectively as possible over the two issues of the candidate's motivation and his 'fitting in', the assessor will reach conclusions which will range between the two extremes of a burning 'yes' and a vehement 'no'. The wise selector will then weigh his findings against his assessment of the verifiable data, and pronounce accordingly. Some organisations require that assessors justify their final decisions in a further narrative panel on the assessment form. It is to be hoped that the justification will be limited to narrative, for very few interviewers are qualified to assess such subjective characteristics as motivation in a more definitive manner.

The reader will note that I have omitted to mention the traits of reliability, initiative, leadership and so on. Once again, I would offer that most of us are just not qualified to formally assess these esoteric qualities. A candidate's working history will demonstrate how and to what extent he has achieved success — verify the data and leave it at that.

Self-tutorial

1 Carry out a critical examination of the interview assessment form illustrated in Figure 8. What further key items might have been included within Part A to enable a more comprehensive assessment to be made of verifiable data?

2 Compile a job specification for your own job — Chapter 2 sets out the main points to be covered — and then draw up an interview assessment form relevant to the post.

3 Finally, have a shot at *appraising yourself* on the assessment form — you may have quite a surprise.

*Gamesmanship or, The Art of Winning Games
Without Actually Cheating.*

Stephen Potter, Book title

8

PRACTICE AND CRIBBING MAKES PERFECT

'The interview was a bit of a farce from beginning to end. The chap started off by saying that he would tell me a little about the organisation — and then didn't stop talking for about twenty-five minutes. Mind you, it was very interesting — I got a complete lecture on how the company acted as agents for these foreign air forces, details on their organisation structure and so on. But, as time wore on and he showed no signs of coming to a halt, I got a bit worried — to tell the truth, I thought I'd better start asking some questions. I posed a couple of queries — I couldn't just sit there like a lemon — but it only made things worse! He just went on and on until, almost in desperation, I had to say, "Is there anything you would like to ask me, Mr English?" Do you know what he said? Something like, "No, I don't think so — your application was very comprehensive and has all the details I need" — you could have knocked me over with a feather! He then said that he'd forgotten to tell me about the air force head-quarters — in which I would be working.... He described the set-up in detail and, quite honestly, used the phrase "You will find..." so often that I was convinced I'd got the job. The whole thing lasted for over an hour and, during that time, the only question he asked was one concerning my health. His parting words were something like, "I hope I've put you in the picture on what you can expect". Three weeks later I got a letter rejecting me — and I'll never know whether it was because he thought I was a dummy at the interview. Interview? I couldn't get a word in edgeways...".'

(Description by a candidate of an interview for a foreign air force appointment)

'... the trouble was that he kept on drying up. I suppose he was shy or something, but — whatever it was — it didn't help things. There were these damned great pauses all the time. I thought he was waiting for me to say something but, when I started to speak, almost every time he'd interrupt with some question he'd suddenly thought of....'

(Reference by a candidate to an interview for a management trainee post)

'He had my application form in front of him and, for the first half of the interview, all that happened was that he went through every item on the form. Not asking me about what I'd put down, mark you, but reading it out — bit by bit — and then asking me if each bit was correct! When he got to the end of the form, he got a bit flustered and seemed stuck for something to ask — so he went back over the details and just asked the odd question here and there. I don't think he learned much about me....'

(Reference by a candidate to an interview for a secretarial post)

'...There were times when I thought I was interviewing him....'

(Reference by a candidate to an interview for a company accountant post)

'... One minute she'd ask me about my hobbies and the next minute about my last job — dodging around like a blue-arsed fly....'

(Reference by a candidate to an interview for a machinist's job)

During the course of my day-to-day lecturing commitments, I always try to profit by the coffee breaks and sound out the opinions of course members on various topics. One of my favourite questions is, 'No names, no pack-drill — but tell me about your last interview for a job. What did you think of the interviewer and how did the session go?' Almost invariably, the replies are couched in adverse vein. This, of course, is proof of what we all know — but are reluctant to admit. By and large, we are lousy interviewers. Throughout this book I have endeavoured to highlight some of our interviewing sins — of commission and omission — but merely reading what I have said is not enough. The adage must be

PRACTISE AND PRACTISE AGAIN — AND AGAIN...

So — how do we practise?

The average manager — there's a term for you — is not blessed with a horde of interview guinea-pigs on which to rehearse his piece. Whilst he may increase his *experience* during the course of interviewing actual candidates — which may, of course, be at fairly sporadic or even rare intervals — he should certainly not subject them to his efforts at early *practice*. What, then, can he do?

First, set his self-training house in order and establish some priorities. I suggest the following simple and progressive steps:

1   Thoroughly digest and learn the various techniques and suggestions outlined in the preceding chapters.
2   Then, and only then, proceed to indoctrinate himself with the form and sequence of questions in the typical employment interview.

There is one further stage — I will deal with this later in the chapter.

The form and sequence of questions

There follows a fairly comprehensive list of open-ended questions. They range from those that would be used in the interview of a young person to others that would only apply to the older, more mature candidate. The purpose of this list is not to offer a text which must be learned by heart but, rather, to provide a useful collection of questions — arranged in a logical sequence — to enable the reader to familiarise himself with question form and sequence. *Study the questions carefully.* Think up possible answers and use your imagination to compose further questions which might be prompted by such replies.

A selection of open-ended questions

1   Let's start at the beginning — when were you born?
2   So — exactly how old are you?
3   Where were you born?
4   Where else have you lived?
5   Where is your home now?
6   How long have you lived there?
7   What do you think of that neighbourhood?
8   What is your father's occupation?
9   What does that entail?
10   What did he do before that?
11   What does your mother do?
12   How many are there in your family?
13   What does that consist of?
14   What does he/she do for a living?
15   Where do you fit in the family?
16   What are your views on marriage?
17   What plans do you have regarding marriage?
18   How did you meet him/her?
19   How did that come about?
20   Let's turn to your schooling — when did you first go to school?
21   What school was that?
22   What age were you when you transferred to secondary schooling?
23   How did that change come about?
24   What choice of school did you have at that stage?
25   How long were you at that school?
26   So — what dates would that be?
27   What other schools have you attended?
28   How far was it from your home to school?
29   How did you journey to and fro?
30   Tell me — how many pupils were there at school?
31   How many boys/girls?
32   What about the classes — how many were there?
33   How were they streamed?
34   What examinations were available at your school?
35   Which examinations did you take?
36   When was that?
37   What were your results?
38   When did you take any other exams?
39   What were the results?
40   What about 'A' Levels — when did you take them?
41   Why did you not sit them?
42   How many subjects did you take?
43   What were the subjects?

44 What grades did you get?
45 Let's change the subject — what sports were played at your school?
46 Which did you play?
47 Which were you worst at?
48 Why was that?
49 How many soccer/cricket teams were there at school?
50 Which team were you in?
51 What positions did you play?
52 Which section of athletics interested you?
53 Why was that?
54 What was your best achievement in...?
55 Turning back to school organisation — how did the pupils help in running the school?
56 How were the prefects chosen?
57 How did you get on with the prefects?
58 Would you have liked to have been a prefect?
59 What duties did that involve you in?
60 What improvements would you have made in the prefect system, had you been given the chance?
61 How was punishment administered at your school?
62 What did you think of this system?
63 Leaving the question of discipline then — what clubs and societies were available at school?
64 Which interested you?
65 What part did you play in...?
66 What did that involve?
67 How long did that take you?
68 What did you have to do?
69 Outside school — what youth organisations were there in your area?
70 Which interested you?
71 Why was that?
72 What part did you play in...?
73 What did that involve?
74 How much of your time did that take up?
75 What did you have to do?
76 How long were you a member of ...?
77 How large was the...?
78 Who actually ran the...?
79 How were you involved in the actual running of...?
80 Now — apart from all this, what else did you do in your spare time?
81 How did this come about?
82 What type of models do you build?

83 Why do you specialise in this way?
84 What was your most successful model?
85 What advice would you offer a beginner in this hobby?
86 Where did you get the money for your hobby/activity?
87 How did you supplement your pocket money?
88 How long did you have that job?
89 What did you earn?
90 What did you have to do?
91 What did you do with the money you earned?
92 How did you spend the school holidays?
93 Where did you go?
94 How did this come about?
95 Who organised it?
96 What of importance have we missed out of your school days?
97 After you left school, what happened then?
98 What prompted this decision?
99 What kind of advice did you take?
100 How many applications for jobs did you make?
101 What did you do at this firm?
102 What did this entail?
103 What was your weekly pay/salary when you joined this firm?
104 What was it when you left them?
105 What do you think was the least enjoyable part of your work
    at this firm?
106 How long were you with the company?
107 What was promotion like in your department?
108 How did you fare?
109 What benefits, other than pay, did you enjoy?
110 Why did you leave?
111 What do you think was the real reason for your dismissal?
112 Looking back, what changes would you have made in your
    career?
113 What other activities are you involved in just now?
114 Thinking of your employment history, I recall from your
    application form that you may have missed out a period. What
    happened from........ to ....?
115 Tell me — what brought this about?
116 I believe you are married — how big is your family?
117 What does your wife do?
118 How old are your children?
119 What formal qualifications do you have?
120 Briefly — how does one qualify as/for...?
121 How did you go about this?
122 How much time did this take?
123 What is the present subscription for ...?

124 Where did you study...?
125 What did that entail?
126 What plans and ambitions do you have for the future?
127 How do you intend to achieve...?
128 How do you envisage our vacancy fitting in with your plans?
129 If offered the post, how would you travel to and fro?
130 What driving experience have you?
131 What car do you run at present?
132 What driving experience has your wife achieved?
133 How much notice are you required to give your present employer?
134 When would you be free to take up new employment?
135 Have you any questions you would like to ask me?

I would like to repeat that the questions should be studied carefully. In thinking up possible answers, it will become apparent that the replies by candidates will often dictate the course of ensuing questions. We are back to the business of the interview going off at a tangent and, at worst, the interviewer losing control of the session. Side-issues and points of interest must be probed, but the interviewer should always be in command of the situation and *steer the discussion.*

Practice — the final stage

I hope that the 135 open-ended questions I have listed will illustrate one slightly sinister point; namely, that the task of posing the right questions — those that will yield profitable answers — requires some effort and experience. As I have already stated, there may not be a horde of interview guinea-pigs available — but there are a few on tap. I refer, of course, to that long-suffering and patient group, the family. Make certain that they understand the business of open-ended questions and then, as a probably welcome respite from television, persuade each member to play the part of candidate. Take care that the sessions do not degenerate into curt interrogations — remember all the rules of the game — and I promise that the results will be very encouraging. Once the technique of asking the right questions has been fairly well mastered, test the newly acquired skill in other situations. For example, have a quiet and careful shot at steering the next conversation in the local — but do exercise a bit of caution, or there may be a sudden dearth of drinking partners.

So — the final stage — practise, again and again.

The gentle art of cribbing

Unlike examinations, the use of cribs in interviewing is an honourable estate. The *modus operandi* is simplicity itself and can be a life-saver for the inexperienced interviewer. Take your desk name-plate — no interviewer worth his salt would be without one — and, on the reverse side, stick your neatly printed crib:

What	Birth	Education	Outside Sch.	Job
When	When	Exams	Hobbies	Duties
Why	Where	Sch. org.	Pin-money	Plans
Where	Homes	Prefects	Holidays	Why left
Which	Family	Clubs	Career plan	Marital
How	Father	Sport	Action taken	Ambitions

Obviously, the crib should be tailored to one's individual needs, with trigger words that are instantly recognisable to the user. It goes without saying that the device is not suitable for use in the informal interview situation, when a desk is not part of the scenario. However, I would strongly recommend that the inexperienced interviewer gains his laurels behind the psychological shelter of his desk, and not over a coffee table. One thing is certain, with the name-plate in the normal position on the desk and assuming the interviewer is not completely myopic, the candidate will not realise a crib is in use.

Get to it — and good interviewing.

Self-tutorial (Part One)

A FINAL INTERVIEW CHECKLIST

1 Put the candidate at ease by commencing the interview in a conversational way with fairly general remarks — *opening gambits.*

2 Maintain a friendly and reasonably informal manner — *a good rapport.*

3 Encourage the candidate to talk by asking the right questions — *open-ended questions.*

4 Plan the ground to be covered in advance — *the chronological main stream.*

5   Probe to uncover details — *a comprehensive and accurate background investigation.*

6   Look for success — *an achiever is an achiever is an achiever.*

7   Identify weaknesses — thorough *perception and prediction.*

8   Know your own limitations — *innate subjectivity!*

9   A perfect interview is worthless if the assessment is faulty — *re-read Chapter 7!*

Self-tutorial (Part Two)

Cribs are not allowed at this stage. Armed with pen, paper and your word of honour attempt to provide detailed answers to the following questions. When you have finished — and not before — check your answers by seeking out the relevant sections in the preceding chapters. There is no time limit, which should be of some consolation . . . .

1   What are open-ended questions?

2   Give two examples of standard-revealing questions.

3   Describe the following interviewing faults:
     Halo Error
     Error of Leniency

4   Why is the timing of interviews crucial to the process?

5   Describe the following:
     Job description
     Job specification

6   What steps would you take to ensure that the reception of interview candidates is adequate and a credit to your firm?

7   What are the golden rules for effective short-listing?

8   During the course of an interview, you find that there are good grounds for doubting the candidate's honesty and you decide to reject him for the post. How would you go about terminating the interview?

9   One of a candidate's stated interests is 'underwater archaeology' — and you have doubts about this. Describe how you would probe for the truth.

10   What are the aims of effective employment advertising?

But I grow old always learning many things.

**Solon (c.640 — c.558 BC), quoted by Herodotus
in 'Histories'**

9

HOME COOKING IS BEST – AN IN- COMPANY INTER- VIEWING COURSE

Bosses and training officers, this chapter is directed mainly at you – which is not to say that more general readers will fail to derive benefit from its contents. I am assuming with some egotism that, having read thus far, those with training responsibilities will be giving a little thought to the question of providing interviewing courses for members of their own organisation. What, then, are the opportunities?

1   Selected executives could attend on of the many 'employment interviewing seminars' currently available on the commercial bandwagon. These are usually of one day's duration and, with fees and expenses, will set the company coffers back by a pretty bob or two for each individual. The delegates – and I say this with the benefit of bitter hindsight – will return to the fold bemused with undigested information and little richer for the experience.

2   Executives could attend one of the few full-length interviewing courses available, usually of 2-3 weeks' duration. Company accountants would be required to find several hundred pounds for individual course fees. The sheer expense will prevent most organisations – management consultants excepted, of course – from allowing their managers to attend these excellent training courses.

3   Be a devil – do your own thing.

It is not only feasible but in many ways desirable that an organisation should run its own interviewing course. Not only will the cost be minimised, but the entire function will be directly controlled by the organisation. The programme content will be restricted to exactly that which the company requires — an important point when money, however much, is being spent on training. It is the aim of this chapter to persuade and convince the reader that a company interviewing course is a viable and worthwhile proposition. So, without further ado, let us proceed to the meat in the sandwich.

That which follows is a complete recipe — a course programme supported by fully detailed notes on item content, presentation and administrative direction. Firstly, however, there are a few essential preliminaries:

Course duration   The course is designed to run over a long weekend, i.e. from Friday evening to tea-time on Sunday. This may shake the sacrosanct views held by some managers, but the fact remains that a weekend is the time when executives can best be spared from their normal duties. Please be warned, the programme should *not* be split into modules for presentation as and when convenient — it simply will not work.

Course size   The programme is designed for an ideal number of fifteen delegates. Many more or less than this number will endanger the smooth running and efficacy of the syllabus.

Course venue   The course is based on the principle of 'total immersion'. Quite simply, it is a residential training session and delegates must be removed from the company environment and other distractions. The question of accommodation is covered in detail later in this chapter.

Directing staff   The programme is intended for presentation by one lecturer-cum-tutor with, ideally, one or two assistants. Again, I will deal with the question of directing staff later on.

A MANAGEMENT COURSE ON EFFECTIVE INTERVIEWING

PROGRAMME

Time	Item	Refer to Note No.
Friday		
18.00 – 19.00	*Delegates arrive* Reception and allocation of rooms – distribution of course folders and name badges	Admin 1
19.30 – 20.00	*A welcoming drink* Delegates gather at bar – meet managing director and course director	Admin 2
20.00 –	*Dinner* Short address by managing director – course director introduces:	Trng 1
	Exercise Ice-breaker Delegates give short self-introductions	Trng 2
	Briefing Course director gives short briefing on programme for next morning	
Saturday		
08.15 – 09.00	*Breakfast*	Admin 3
09.00 – 09.45	*An introduction to selection interviewing* Traditional approaches, misconceptions and fallibilities – the interview as a selection tool – getting factors into their proper perspective	Trng 4
09.45 – 10.30	*Paving the way for an effective interview* Job specifications – interpretation of candidates' applications – short-listing – arranging the interview	Trng 5
10.30 – 10.45	*Morning coffee*	Admin 4

(continued overleaf)

Time	Item	Refer to Note No.

Time	Item	Refer to Note No.
10.45 – 11.30	*The technique of interview questioning* Open-ended questions v. direct questions – standard-revealing questions – wrong attitudes – controlling the interview.	Trng 6
	Exercise Question Mark Delegates complete an exercise on questioning technique	Trng 7
11.30 – 12.30	*Exercise Dead Cert* Delegates complete an exercise on the interpretation of information on candidates	Trng 8
12.30 – 14.00	*Lunch*	Admin 5
14.00 – 14.30	*The interview environment* Timing and reception of candidates – the interview room – formal and informal sessions – adverse conditions	Trng 9
14.30 – 15.15	*The technique of interview questioning (continued)* Rogues cheats and vagabonds – the art of the probe – references – a miscellany of cautions	Trng 10
15.15 – 15.30	*Afternoon tea*	Admin 6
15.30 – 16.30	*Assessing the candidate* Weighing the facts – assessment methods – pitfalls – a suggested approach – motivation and other intangibles	Trng 11
16.30 – 17.15	*Exercise Mark-up* Delegates witness an interview and complete an interview assessment on the candidate	Trng 12
17.15 – 19.00	*Course break*	Admin 7
19.00 – 19.45	*Dinner*	Admin 8

Time	Item	Refer to. Note No.
19.45 – 20.15	*Exercise Mark-up (continued)* Analysis of delegates' assessments and discussion	Trng 12
20.15 – 21.00	*Exercise briefing for the following day* In addition to briefing, delegates are given the opportunity for re-cap on events to date — in preparation for Exercise Deep End	Trng 13

Sunday

Time	Item	Refer to. Note No.
08.30 – 09.30	*Breakfast*	Admin 9
09.30 – 12.00 (approx)	*Exercise Deep End* Delegates form syndicates and each member carries out an interview (preferably two) of a young person — morning coffee available during session	Trng 14 Admin 10
12.00 – 13.00 (approx)	*Exercise Deep End De-brief* Delegates and young interviewees meet and discuss in open forum — summing-up by the course director	Trng 15
13.00 – 14.30 (approx)	*Lunch* — young interviewees as guests	Admin 11
14.30 – 15.15	*Re-Cap and Open Forum* The young interviewees having departed, the course director gives a frank re-cap on Exercise Deep End — questions	Trng 16
15.15 – 16.00	*Exercise Belly Laugh* Delegates participate in a 'surprise package' exercise	Trng 17
16.00	*Delegates depart*	Admin 12

A note on the notes

The administrative and training notes listed against each programme item are, in fact, the detailed instructions for the successful implementation of the programme as a whole. Read on and cross-refer.

Training notes

Trng 1   *Opening address by managing director*   I hope it will be obvious that the active interest of the company's big brass is a prerequisite to the success of the course. I might add that senior management probably need the training as much as their subordinates — senior executive readers and training officers, please take note. The after-dinner address by the managing director should proceed — hopefully with injections of wit and pleasantry — along the following lines:

'We in common with most companies.... rely upon the employment interview as the sole means of selecting staff.... and make the fatal assumption that company executives are capable of conducting a searching interview.... without previous training in the technique.... you will find that this course.... proves the point in inescapable terms.... proceeds to a study of employment interviewing procedures.... together with sophisticated but down-to-earth practical exercises.... make no apology for dragging you away from your homes.... because I am quite confident that the weekend's very hard work will prove stimulating.... instructive.... and quite out of the ordinary.... I now introduce.... course director....'

Brief address by course director   This should be *very* brief. Reference should be made to the course programme — already distributed to delegates (see note Admin 1), and Exercise Ice-Breaker should be introduced:

'.... one secret of success of this type of course.... that all the delegates get to know one another.... for this purpose.... like to ask each one of you to introduce yourself.... quite informally, without leaving your seat.... merely take two minutes or so.... include details of your appointment and function.... very brief personal history.... let me kick off.... I am....'

The course director should 'help the proceedings along' – ensuring, for example, that shy delegates are not left in stumbling silence during their self-introductions. *The flow and climate of this inaugural dinner is all-important to the smooth running of the course.* Particular attention should be paid to the points made in note Admin 2.

Trng 2 *Exercise Ice-Breaker*   All self-introductions should be limited to about two minutes' duration. Ensure that the 'crib' on place name cards (see note Admin 2) is available.

Trng 3 *Briefing for next day*   Refer to domestic arrangements – bar facilities, telephones, need for early start – be prompt for breakfast. Essential that delegates assemble in course room – give location – at 09.00 precisely. Inform delegates that the bar is now open and mention any other facilities that are available.

Trng 4 AN INTRODUCTION TO SELECTION INTERVIEWING

Prior to start   Ensure that place-names have been allocated as previously arranged – having observed during the last night's dinner any 'awkward cliques', etc. Have OHP 1 (a reference to the appropriate overhead projector transparency – see OHP list at the end of these notes) *already illuminated* when delegates arrive. Make no comment on OHP 1 – merely remove when session starts.

Content   Use the contents of Chapter 1 as a basis for lecture notes:
1   Expand theme of ineffective interviews with personal or concocted accounts – try to achieve some light-hearted references.
2   Expand theme of 'errors' with real or concocted examples. Remember that one method used to illustrate the fallibility of humans to assess other people is –
'Group of people are shown a selected feature film.

They are invited to pay particular attention to certain characters in the film. At the conclusion, those present are invited to "rate" the characters, using a simple rating form. Massive divergence of opinion always results.'

3   Show OHP 4 and describe significance of ratings — no consensus of opinion.
4   Expand and discuss types of information usually investigated — skill, experience, etc.
5   Utilise the quiz at the end of Chapter 1 as a basis for questioning and discussion.

Remember that this session — as with all other sessions — requires a two-way exchange. The course must be participatory.

Training aids   In addition to OHP's 1 and 4, it is recommended that attractive transparencies be prepared listing the errors and the types of information usually investigated. OHP list for some tips in the preparation of transparencies.

Lecture hand-outs are required. These should be attractively produced and brief in content. Do not distribute the hand-outs until the session is concluded — but mention the fact that *brief* hand-outs will be made available.

Trng 5   PAVING THE WAY FOR AN EFFECTIVE INTERVIEW

Content   Use the contents of Chapter 2 as a basis for lecture notes:

1   Expand theme of job descriptions, specifications — distribute examples.
2   Expand advertising theme by distributing — or showing on OHP transparencies — examples of good and bad ads. Play tape recording of dramatised version of employer ordering insertion of advertisement.
3   Distribute copies of completed CVs and application forms to support points made in lecture. Invite delegates to spot salient points in the examples.
4   Utilise the quiz and parts of the self-tutorial at the end of Chapter 2 to generate questions and discussion.

Training aids   Tape recorder (see above) and selected OHPs. Completed CVs and applications. Lecture hand-outs.

Trng 6   THE TECHNIQUE OF INTERVIEW QUESTIONING

Content   Use the contents of Chapter 5 as a basis for lecture notes:

1   Expand theme of questioning technique by demonstration of points made − a playlet using assistant in the role of interviewee *or* by tape recording. Ensure that points are illustrated 'larger than life'.
2   Invite delegates to do written exercise on interview questions − using example in Chapter 5 as basis for this, see *Trng 7*, below.
3   OHPs should be produced which highlight all types of interview questions and attitudes.

Training aids   Tape recorder and selected OHPs. Exercise blanks (see below). Lecture hand-outs.

Trng 7   EXERCISE QUESTION MARK

The exercise paper should be produced with blank spaces beneath each item to enable delegates to write in their answers. Allow approximately 15 minutes for delegates to answer, say, 15 questions − but monitor progress carefully and time accordingly. Carry out 'round-robin' check of results, using the 'name last' technique − 'What do you have for answer no. 10, Michael?'

Trng 8   EXERCISE DEAD CERT

This is a 'paper exercise' in which delegates are supplied with detailed case histories of two mythical candidates. Following study of the data, delegates are invited to make, and be prepared to justify, selection decisions. An example of such an exercise follows.

Instructions to delegates   You are asked to study the case histories of two applicants for the mythical post of

Personnel Officer. The job specification for the appointment is as follows:

Age   25-30 years.
Qualifications   Ideally, BA in Business Studies (sandwich course), membership of Institute of Personnel Management.
Previous experience   All-round experience in junior personnel post within a large organisation. Practical experience in industrial relations, with emphasis on industrial tribunal case preparation and progression.
Special requirements   Above-average powers of written and verbal expression. Successful applicant will be required to travel extensively − company car provided. Should have promotion potential − intended that successful applicant will replace Personnel Manager on retirement in two years' time. Should be willing to undergo further training − courses at Ashridge College, etc., envisaged.

The following case histories contain information derived from the candidates' application forms, from questioning at preliminary interviews and from certain referees. You are invited to study the information and make some selection decisions.

WILLIAM LEE

Lee is the only son of a provincial bank manager who was forced to retire prematurely following a serious operation for brain tumour, which has left him almost totally disabled. Aged 26 years, Lee underwent a state schooling and achieved 'O' Level passes in English Language, English Literature, Mathematics, History, Geography, Physics and Art. Just before leaving school at the age of 18½ years, Lee obtained 'A' Level passes in English Literature, Mathematics and Physics. He then entered a local Polytechnic as a full-time student and subsequently gained the Higher National Diploma in Business Studies. As a schoolboy, Lee was not very interested in organised games and did not shine in cricket or football. He excelled as an athlete, however, and was Victor Ludorum at three consecutive school sports days. He was a founder member of the school debating society and, for two years, secretary to the local youth club. On gaining his HND, Lee applied for and obtained a post with a local firm as personal assistant to the managing director — a post which he has held for some 3½ years. The preliminary interview report on Lee included the following narrative notes:

'Lee agrees that his career to date has been influenced by his father's disability — he appears to have taken his obligations to his parents very seriously. He now states, however, that — after considerable thought and discussion with his parents, he wishes to embark on a career in personnel management and is not concerned over the prospect of enforced mobility. It is clear that he enjoys a marked proficiency in verbal communication — at interview, he impressed me with his relaxed manner, his polite but forthright comments and replies, and his common sense. He is a student member of the IPM and is halfway through a part-time college course in personnel management. Whilst Lee was neatly and properly dressed for the interview, I have to admit that his appearance worried me. Whilst — as I have said — he spoke in a relaxed manner, his face remained unsmiling and tense in expression. His hair is unruly, his eyes are deep-set in dark hollows, his skin is rough and scarred with past acne disorders and he has a sallow complexion.'

The reference from Lee's current boss contains the following comments:

'I am aware that Lee is seeking an alternative post, preferably in personnel management, and I wish him every success. I might add that there is no suitable opening for him within this company, and I cannot expect a young man of his calibre to remain content with his present lot as my PA. I have found him very successful at his job; he takes his work very seriously indeed and I have been virtually unable to fault him in matters of judgement or application. He thrives on challenging situations and, although inclined to be argumentative at times, acquits himself well.'

MAURICE BROWNLOW

Brownlow is aged 31 years and is married with one baby son. He attended a grammar school and has 'O' Levels in English Language, English Literature, Mathematics and History. On leaving school at 16, he went to work as a junior clerk in the general office of a small engineering firm. Eighteen months later, Brownlow changed his job and became a general clerk within the personnel department of a multinational chemical processing organisation. A year later, he left this job and joined another engineering company, again as a clerk within the personnel department. This company is his present employer and he has completed over twelve years service with the firm. Shortly after joining the company, he attended day release at the local technical college and obtained his Ordinary National Certificate in Business Studies. On his fourth anniversary with the company, he was promoted to the post of personnel office supervisor – an appointment which he held for just over two years. He was then promoted to assistant personnel manager – his current appointment. He has attended numerous short courses in personnel and general management and has been an Associate Member of the IPM for eighteen months. His company is a heavily unionised organisation and, in addition to general personnel work, he has had considerable practical experience in industrial relations. Brownlow's current leisure interests include boating – he has built his own small cruiser from scratch – and amateur dramatics. The preliminary interview report on Brownlow included the following comments:

'The candidate arrived late for the interview, apologising for the fact that his car had broken down. This initial setback was not ameliorated by my impression of his appearance. Brownlow was casually dressed – he wore what I believe is termed a safari suit, together with a rather gaudy shirt and tie. I cannot say he was untidy but I did not deem his choice of attire to be suited to the occasion. A tall, athletic figure with imposing features, he gave me the impression that – given the chance – he would dominate the interview. I cannot fault his career with his current employers – Brownlow has clearly done well to achieve his present position.'

A reference from Brownlow's immediate boss contains the following comments:

'Maurice is seeking advancement in personnel management and rightly deserves to make further progress — which is unfortunately not possible within this company. He is a highly popular and effective manager, and he has coped particularly well with a more than average load of industrial relations problems.'

COMPARISON

Lee and Brownlow, in common with other applicants for the post of Personnel Officer, were given an 'employment questionnaire' to complete. Some of their answers were as follows:

Question	Lee	Brownlow
Do you ever find yourself questioning the policies and directions of your superiors?	No	Yes
Have you ever sensed that you were unpopular with your subordinates?	No	Yes
Do you believe that a personnel manager should represent himself as an impartial figure — rather than as a 'company man' through and through?	Yes	No
It is often said that 'people are a company's most valuable asset' — would you agree?	Yes	No

Your task

1   Complete the starred items on the following interview profile form. Note that some items have already been completed for you by the insertion of the relevant

INTERVIEW PROFILE FORM

Name of candidate .....*Lee & Brownlow*..... Your Name ....

		Low		Average		High	
		1	2	3	4	5	6

Manner and appearance

Speech						B	L
Features ✳							
Dress						B	L
Courtesy ✳							

Sociability

Experience in teamwork ✳							
Participation in group affairs	L	B					

Emotional stability

Calm, unraffled disposition		LB					
Competent manner & approach ✳							
Will accept criticism		LB					

Leadership capacity

Leadership experience ✳							
Evidence of natural leadership traits ✳							

Note to delegates: This interview profile form is the product of the imaginary company featured in this exercise. You should *not* consider it in any other light.

SELECTION DECISION FORM

When you have completed the interview profile form, please deal with these additional points:

1   Indicate your selection decision with a tick:

    a   I would select *Lee* with a high degree of confidence . . . .

    b   I would select *Brownlow* with a high degree of confidence . . . .

    c   I would select *Lee,* but not with great confidence . . . .

    d   I would select *Brownlow,* but not with great confidence . . . .

    e   I would not select either of them . . . .

2   Please state briefly what alternative action you would take (if any) in order to ease your selection task in this case.

. . . .

. . . .

. . . .

. . . .

. . . .

. . . .

initial (Lee – 'L', Brownlow – 'B') in the rating boxes
You should record your findings in the same way.

2   Complete the selection decision form, which follows
the profile form.

Exercise Dead Cert is plainly intended to provoke discussion
amongst delegates. The course director should ensure that
this discussion is steered to include interpretation of
candidates' data and the fallibility of selectors' opinion and
assumption. Needless to say, there is no 'correct answer' to
the exercise, but full advantage should be taken by the
course director to probe delegates' decisions and to offer
constructive criticism where necessary.

Trng 9   THE INTERVIEW ENVIRONMENT

Content   Use the contents of Chapter 3 as a basis for
lecture notes:

1   Expand theme by persuading delegates to offer
accounts of personal experiences, suggestions
concerning other advantages, disadvantages, etc.
2   Induce a discussion on the question of formal/
informal interview sessions, the ethics of selection
'tricks' in interviewing.
3   Compose a questionnaire on the lines of the
employers' checklist at the end of Chapter 3 – use
this as a quiz during the session.

Training aids   Lecture hand-outs and quiz blanks.

Trng 10   THE TECHNIQUE OF INTERVIEW QUESTIONING
(CONTINUED)

Content   Use the contents of Chapter 6 as a basis for
lecture notes:

1   Expand the theme of probing by inviting delegates
to investigate statements made by colleagues, i.e.
get one course member to name a hobby (actual or
imaginary) and invite another delegate to probe for
the truth.
2   Produce and distribute examples of references –
discuss the validity of the examples.

3   Produce for inspection examples of forged documents.

Training aids   Examples of references and forged documents. Lecture hand-outs.

Trng 11   ASSESSING THE CANDIDATE

Content   Use the contents of Chapter 7 as a basis for lecture notes:

1   Use the experience of Exercise Dead Cert as an introductory theme to the session.
2   Produce examples of assessment forms similar to those illustrated in Chapter 7 — provoke discussion and invite delegates to argue against assessment forms in general. Course director, beware! Have your big guns at the ready!
3   Produce OHPs similar to Figures 4-5 to illustrate methods of assessment.
4   Produce an OHP similar to Figure 8 to illustrate a suggested approach to assessment. Distribute copies of this assessment form and invite delegates to carry out the tasks set in the self-tutorial to Chapter 7.

Training aids   Selected OHPs. Examples of assessment forms and suggested form. Lecture hand-outs.

Trng 12   EXERCISE MARK-UP

The course director and his assistant — or, for that matter, any willing, able and *well-rehearsed* volunteers — should present a convincing playlet of an interview lasting for 25-30 minutes. This will require careful preparation, for it is important that the session does not contain any 'bloomers' in technique or presentation. Delegates should be invited to complete a full assessment of the candidate. They should also be told that, after dinner, a critique of their efforts will take place, when every opportunity will be given for them to justify their decisions.

The assessment forms should be collected at the end of the session and it is then up to the course director to sweat blood preparing his critique in readiness for the session at 19.45.

Trng 13   EXERCISE BRIEFING FOR THE FOLLOWING DAY

For the purposes of this exercise, which represents the culmination of the weekend's work, it is necessary to carry out some purposeful liaison with the headmaster of the senior school situated nearest to the course venue. The object is to obtain his approval and support for the 'casual hire' of *six* of the best sixth-form pupils to act as interview guinea-pigs. It will be found – and I can confirm this from personal experience – that if the objects of the interviewing course are explained, headmasters are very willing to participate in the venture. The youngsters concerned will, of course, derive valuable experience from their interviews – and, it is to be hoped, a little extra pin-money, plus lunch on the firm.

So far as the briefing is concerned, delegates should be told that – on the morrow – they will be interviewing real, live candidates. It should be explained that the young people will *not* have received any coaching and will probably be just as anxious as the interviewers themselves. The delegates should also be told that each youngster will complete an application form, as if he or she were applying for an actual job, and that these completed forms will be available for the interviewers' use.

The course director should make a point of assuaging the very definite qualms that will arise with some delegates, and encourage questions and recapitulation of points covered in the course.

Trng 14   EXERCISE DEEP END

Procedure   The following procedure should be followed:
1   Ensure that the young people arrive in good time for the exercise and that they have brought their application forms with them. It will be necessary to photostat these for distribution to delegates.
2   Divide the delegates into three syndicates – one syndicate will use the main course room and the other two groups will utilise the two syndicate rooms.
3   The first round of interviews – to last for 25 minutes each – will entail the first three youngsters being interviewed. The second round will entail these same three youngsters going for second interviews in

different rooms — and, on the third round, a similar switch-over. The fourth and ensuing rounds will be carried out by the second group of youngsters. In other words, *each delegate will carry out one interview* and *witness* (in the case of five-member syndicates) *four carried out by his colleagues.* Each will be interviewed several times — *but never in the same room.*

4   During the exercise, the directing staff should circulate quietly making notes for subsequent use in the de-briefing. Plainly, there will have to be a waiting-place for the youngsters who are not being interviewed — and the directing staff should make a point of visiting this at regular intervals. Again, quiet note should be taken of comments made by the interviewees — for it is certain that quite devastating remarks will be forthcoming.

      If time permits, it is infinitely preferable that each course member should carry out at least two practice interviews — and time should be made to thus permit!

5   The duration of interviews should be watched closely and sessions which threaten to be interminable should be terminated by pleasant interruption. A careful watch should also be maintained for the odd delegate who is plainly unable to cope — there always seems to be at least one such individual on every course.

Trng 15 EXERCISE DEEP END DE-BRIEF

Note that this de-briefing session is conducted in the presence of the young interviewees. The purpose of the discussion is to obtain detailed observations from each youngster — taking due care to ensure that the comments are constructive. It will be found that the calibre of these sixth-formers — in terms of perceptive and penetrating comment — will be surprisingly high. Discussion between the delegates and their young guests should be encouraged, and the directing staff should inject their observations — thereby provoking further comment from both sides. The course director should deliver a lively and encouraging summing-up at the end of the session, and then invite the delegates to take the youngsters for a pre-lunch drink.

Trng 16 RECAP AND OPEN FORUM

The purpose of this session is to enable the directing staff to make any comments on Exercise Deep End which could not be made in the presence of the young interviewees. The session should then be allowed to develop into a general open forum. *The directing staff should ensure that the proceedings end on a congratulatory and cheerful note* — for this is the last formal period of the course.

Trng 17   EXERCISE BELLY LAUGH

It must be said that this final exercise has no other purpose than to send the delegates away from the course on a cheerful but thinking note. It may therefore be regarded as optional — personal experience has shown, however, that it constitutes a flourishing finalé to the weekend.

Background to the exercise   The traditional method of appraising people entails the assessment of subordinates by their superiors. Another method, which breaks with tradition and produces many accurate results, is to require individuals to be assessed by their equals — peer ratings. Exercise Belly Laugh is a light-hearted peer-ratings session.

Procedure   The exercise requires two forms to be produced, as illustrated in the accompanying Figure 9. Delegates are issued with the forms — note that they are required to enter their names on the assessment panel. Once this is done and the smaller form is positioned as shown in the figure, the papers are collected and 'shuffled'. They are then re-issued to delegates, care being taken to ensure that no delegate receives his own forms back. Participants are then invited to rate the individual named on the form by entering — in the first vertical column — *two ticks* for that individual's *most outstanding* qualities, and *two crosses* to represent his *least outstanding* qualities. Delegates then cover up their assessments by re-positioning the small form over the first column — and the forms are then passed on for the next round. This procedure is, of course, repeated until each individual has rated all his colleagues. Obviously, delegates are instructed to ignore their own form when this arrives in front of them.
Once the ratings are completed, the forms are distributed to their owners for their private consideration. The directing staff should emphasise that they do not wish to be made

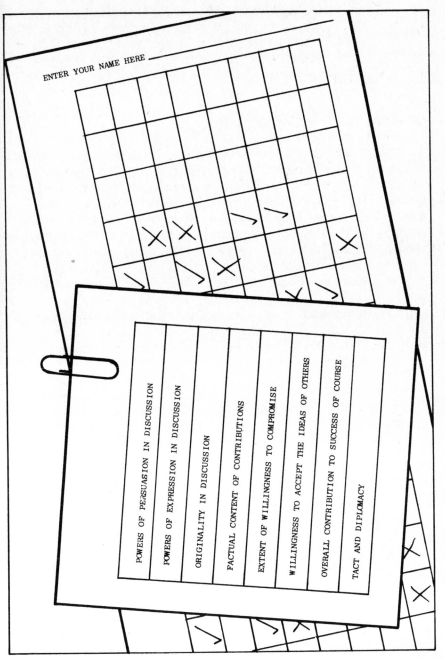

ENTER YOUR NAME HERE

POWERS OF PERSUASION IN DISCUSSION

POWERS OF EXPRESSION IN DISCUSSION

ORIGINALITY IN DISCUSSION

FACTUAL CONTENT OF CONTRIBUTIONS

EXTENT OF WILLINGNESS TO COMPROMISE

WILLINGNESS TO ACCEPT THE IDEAS OF OTHERS

OVERALL CONTRIBUTION TO SUCCESS OF COURSE

TACT AND DIPLOMACY

Figure 9 Exercise Belly Laugh — assessment forms

119

aware of any ratings and that the whole exercise is one of private information only. It should be pointed out that only outstanding strengths and least outstanding strengths have been annotated — and not subjected to assessment as 'bad' (etc.). A consensus of opinion may, or may not, be reflected in the results — this is for individual delegates to decide!

Overhead projector transparencies

The quality of a training course will be partly judged by the standard of the visual aids utilised during the instruction. Every effort should be made to ensure that OHP transparencies are well-drawn, coloured, succinct and relevant to the subject. Unless produced by a skilled artist, all lettering should be carried out by the dry transfer 'instant lettering' method. Ready-cut acetate sheets and cardboard frames can be purchased from any stockist of training materials. Special inks, pens and other colouring mediums can also be obtained. The days of ill-defined, shoddy scrawls passing as OHP transparencies are over.

The OHP transparencies to be used with the interviewing course can be derived from the contents of this book, but the essential choice of material is up to the people concerned. The following list is provided as a practical guide:

OHP 1 Opening gambit — optical illusion (see Figure 10).
OHP 2 Errors — Halo, Logical, etc.
OHP 3 List of qualities — skill, experience, etc.
OHP 4 Typical assessment results (see Figure 1).
OHP 5 Reproductions of 'good' advertisments.
OHP 6 Reproductions of 'poor' advertisements.
OHP 7 'What, why, when...', etc. (see Figure 2).
OHP 8 Typical graphic scale (see Figure 5).
OHP 9 Typical ranking system (see Figure 6).
OHP 10 Typical checklist scale (see Figure 7).
OHP 11 Suggested approach to assessment (see Figure 8).
OHP 12 Exercise Belly Laugh (see Figure 9).

Administrative notes

Admin 1 *Course joining instructions* These should be issued well in advance of the course and should contain all necessary information – details of accommodation, map of the area, course programme, etc.

Reception of delegates   A member of the course staff should meet all delegates and ensure that rooms are allocated without inconvenience. Course folders, containing an additional copy of the programme and a short write-up on the course director's background, should be issued – together with lapel name badges. Delegates should be asked to congregate in the bar at 19.30.

A welcoming gimmick   The very nature of this course demands that, right from the outset, delegates get to know each other and form a friendly, tension-free group. It is well worth spending a little company money to ensure that this is so. One little 'trick' that works wonders in breaking the initial ice is to buy a quantity of magazines – some of the girlie type and some of the Economist variety – and to ensure that each delegate finds one or the other on his bedside table. Small packets of headache pills should also be distributed with the magazines. I guarantee the efficacy of this little gimmick in sparking off conversation at the bar.

Arrangements for the inaugural dinner   Bearing in mind that delegates will have completed a day's work by the time of their arrival and that it is Friday night,

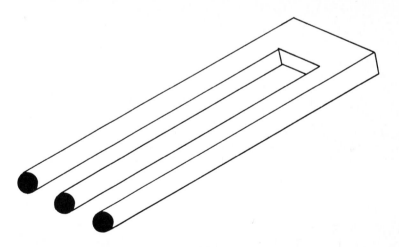

Figure 10   Course opening gambit

particular efforts should be made to ensure that the opening meal is of a high standard.

Admin 2   *Drinks at the bar and the question of payment*   I strongly recommend that the initial gathering at the bar — together with the provision of wine for the two evening meals — is 'on the company'. On all other occasions, delegates should foot their own bill.

The welcoming bar session   The course director, with the able support of senior management, must ensure that this is a pleasantly informal session. It must not be allowed to develop into a mighty thrash and, to this end, it is essential that dinner commences promptly on time.

Seating arrangements at dinner   Places at table should be allocated with artful cunning. Well-known groups should be split up and senior managers dispersed throughout the seating plan. Place cards are essential — if only for the reason that, on the reverse of each card, the following words should appear:

> NAME . . . APPOINTMENT . . . COMPANY/DEPT . . . FAMILY
> VERY BRIEF PERSONAL HISTORY

Admin 3   *Breakfast*   Perhaps this is the appropriate point at which to emphasise the course director's responsibility concerning the punctual timing of all meals. Even the best hotels seem to fall down on this requirement and constant reminders-cum-kicks are vital. Incidentally, the petty cash should run to the provision of newspapers for delegates.

Admin 4   *Coffee and cleaning*   Two points to remember — morning coffee and afternoon tea should be on a serve-yourself basis, and the course room should be tidied up whilst delegates are enjoying their break.

Admin 5   *Lunch*   No place names are required for this or future meals. Ensure that delegates move into the dining room on time — no prolonged bar sessions, particularly at lunchtime.

Admin 6   *Afternoon tea*   This may seem a nit-picking point, but attention to the small details will ensure that complaints or grumbles are minimised — make certain that the 'serve-yourself' tea is hot. Coffee can survive a hot-plate but tea — yuk.

Admin 7   *Course break*   By this time in the programme, delegates will be suffering from an acute lack of fresh air — be sure to recommend a quick walk.

Admin 8   *Dinner*   Whilst this meal should be formal, it is an ideal time to produce, say, a parent board director out of the hat as a guest for the occasion. I have done this on past occasions and, whilst the dear old chap somewhat stupified those present with his anxiety to display an active interest, the delegates generally appreciated the gesture.

Admin 9   *Just a reminder* that delegates will probably be required to clear their rooms during the morning — and that transport is required for those young interviewees.

Admin 10   *Morning coffee*   On this occasion, morning coffee should be freely available throughout the morning. It will be found that delegates and the young interviewees develop remarkable thirsts as a result of their stressful activity.

Admin 11   *Lunch arrangements*   This meal should be a cold buffet, arranged on a serve-yourself basis. The course director should ensure that the young interviewees are placed at ease — and that plenty of food is available.

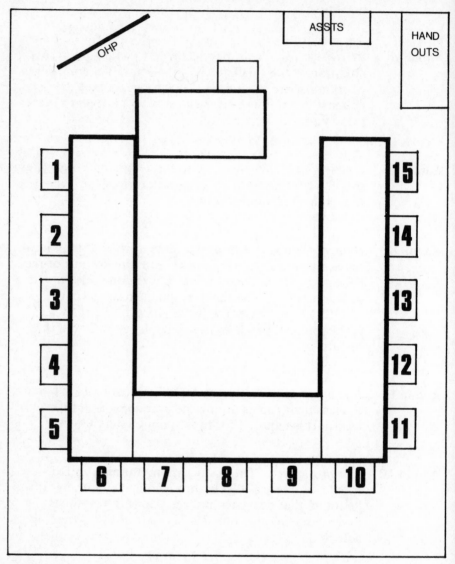

Figure 11 Course accommodation — suggested layout

Admin 12 *The big departure* If some delegates face longish trips home, ensure that afternoon tea is available immediately after the course concludes its final session. See the delegates on their way with all help and assistance — particularly the guy who finds that his car battery is flat.

Course venue

There is a plethora of hotels offering conference and training facilities. There are also more specialist establishments which cater for these activities alone — where the general public does not intrude upon the training scene. One thing is certain, great care must be taken in selecting the course venue — the moral must be to shop around. I have said already that the interviewing course is based upon the principle of total immersion. Private dining facilities — certainly for the opening dinner — and, ideally, a private bar are points to bear in mind. The training accommodation must obviously be of a high standard. Figure 11 illustrates the layout required for a course of fifteen delegates.

Directing staff

Alright — now we come to the crunch. The organisation that possesses a training officer may well have no problem, provided that worthy is of the right calibre to present the interviewing course. If not — or in the event that no training staff are available — then outside help may have to be sought. This is one course which depends for its success on a totally proficient directing staff — there is no short cut. The minimum requirements for the course director are successful completion of a residential and first-class interviewing course, a definite ability to communicate at all levels with a convincing and persuasive manner, and a pronounced enthusiasm for the subject. If, as is my hope, the reader is keen to bring about an improvement of interviewing standards within his organisation — and if he possesses the necessary influence — he will find a way round this problem of acquiring the right person for the job. *In extremis* — why, drop me a line!

Appendix

FURTHER AIDS TO EFFICIENT SELECTION

SELECTION TESTS

The discerning employer, having plugged the gaps in his interviewing defences, may well consider the introduction of some form of objective testing procedure in a further effort to sort out the wheat from the dangerous chaff. The purpose of this appendix is to plonk both feet firmly outside the interviewing arena and provide a very basic introduction to selection tests, an *hors d'oeuvres* on the subject which, hopefully, will whet the appetite and provoke some cost-conscious thought. So – at the risk of teaching you to suck eggs – let me start by listing a few of the areas in which the application of well-validated and inexpensive tests can *vastly improve* the employer's selection armoury:

Clerical recruitment

The assessment of individual speed and accuracy in:

- Checking large lists of numbers and names.
- Filing, classifying and checking data.
- Spelling.
- Arithmetic.

Engineering/mechanical recruitment

Accurate assessment of:

- Mechanical comprehension — the perception and grasp of basic physical and mechanical principles.
- Mechanical information — knowledge of common workshop terms.
- Attainment in arithmetic.
- Spatial perception — the ability to visualize the assembly of two-dimensional geometric shapes into a whole design.
- Manual dexterity — the ability of eye-hand co-ordination.
- Colour blindness — often overlooked at considerable cost.

Recruitment in general

- The assessment of the relative intelligence of an applicant.

The last example merits more detailed comment for, in my experience, whilst managers appreciate the importance of intelligence as a selection yardstick, many have only a hazy perception of what it is all about.

Intelligence and intelligence testing

Alfred Binet and Théodore Simon, two French psychologists who did most of the original work in intelligence testing in the early 1900s, defined intelligence as:

1 An individual's appreciation of a problem, and direction towards its solution.
2 The capacity for making the necessary adaptations to reach an end and the power of self-criticism.

Binet and Simon devised a system of rating the intelligence and mental development of children according to their performance in carefully selected and graded tests, which culminated in the emergence of their best-known and universally accepted work, the

Binet-Simon Scale of Intelligence Quotients (IQ):

$$IQ = \frac{Mental\ Age}{Chronological\ Age} \times 100$$

The crux of the work was, of course, the production and validation of the series of tests completed by the children, with each paper representing the average test that a child of a given age could manage. Thus, for example, the IQ of a child aged six years was derived as follows:

He succeeded at all the 3-year level tests
He succeeded at all the 4-year level tests
He succeeded at all the 5-year level tests
He succeeded at 3/5ths of the 6-year level tests
He succeeded at 1/5th of the 7-year level tests
He failed at all of the 8-year level tests

Since the child passed all of the 5-year level tests, the *base year* is regarded as 6. Thereafter, the child is credited with 1/5th of a year for each correct test, with the result that the *mental age* is:

$$5 + \frac{3}{5} + \frac{1}{5} = 5\frac{4}{5}$$

Therefore, in this example, the child's IQ is:

$$\frac{29 \times 100}{5 \times 6} = 96$$

The average IQ on the Binet-Simon Scale is 100. The reader may be interested to note the following representative examples of other IQ ratings:

IQ of 55 and under — Mentally defective
IQ of 85 and under — The subject will probably benefit from special schooling
IQ of 100 — Average general intelligence
IQ of 110 — Average IQ of arts graduates at one university
IQ of 115 — Average IQ of medicine graduates at one university
IQ of 120 — Average IQ of science graduates at one university
IQ of 145 and over — Very superior ability

| IQ of 150 | — | Not unknown — perhaps once per thousand, which means that, given a population of over 50 million, there are quite a few such gifted people around! |

It is worth noting that intelligence does not appear to change drastically during life, except as a result of accident or illness. It therefore follows that a child who is one year ahead of his group at the age of five will be two years ahead at the age of ten. However, actual growth of intelligence probably ceases fairly early in life, and most of us are probably aware of the sinister statistic which informs us that there is usually a slow, steady decline in intelligence once the 35th year has been left behind. Nevertheless, there is a ray of hope for middle-aged and more senior types, in that the decline can be arrested by changes of activity — when the dear old grey matter rises to the challenge. The man with a high IQ may well be more prone to engage in mental activity and may thus increase his advantage over those with lower IQs.

Since an individual's IQ can be swiftly and accurately assessed by means of intelligence testing, the thinking manager will wish to include the process within his initial selection procedures. He will know from experience that, on some routine jobs, people with an average IQ make better employees than those with high intelligence, who become bored with their lot and seek pastures new. Conversely and if he is frank, our worthy manager will admit that, at some time during his selection forays, he has committed the bloomer of employing a dunderhead — thereby penalising the firm and, it should be remembered, committing an act of gross unfairness against the hapless employee, whose IQ is immutable and a fact of the poor chap's life. Such a manager will be aware of the penetrating and awkward view taken by industrial tribunals when considering dismissals for alleged incompetency:

'If you, as a responsible employer, selected this man because he was suited to the post — why is he not suited to it now?'
Poor selection can, and does, cost a great deal of money. Testing is a sure and certain method of minimising this cost — so think on't!

Can anyone obtain tests?

As I have attempted to illustrate, selection tests are extremely useful to many branches of industry and commerce but — and it is a big but — used by people with inadequate training, they can do more harm than good. Luckily, training takes very little time and is relatively inexpensive — and, for a change, can produce quite dramatic benefits in terms of swift, effective and economic selection. Full details on testing in general and a list of organisations providing recognised training in test administration and interpretation are freely available from the Test Department, NFER Publishing Company, Darville House, 2 Oxford Road East, Windsor, SL4 1DF (Tel: Windsor 69345).

EMPLOYMENT APPLICATION FORMS

The application form is not only the poor old candidate's 'silent ambassador' (and, Gawd knows, that should be sufficient reason for getting the thing right), it is also the vital adjunct to successful and efficient short-listing. Far too many organisations — big and small — pay scant attention to two basic rules for good application form design:

For maximum information, pose 'maximum questions'
For maximum clarity and ease of completion, afford maximum space

'Maximum questions'

Consider, for example, an application form for the selection of 'executive grades' and, in particular, the important 'Employment History' section of such a form. While most organisations allot some priority to the quizzing of candidates in relation to the 'current or most recent appointment', how many go to the lengths of *really* probing the subject? Remember, the candidate who isn't asked will seldom come up with the information — so, try the following for size:

Employer's name, address and telephone number.
Precise job title. *(Too often, the company-allotted 'official' job title is hopelessly vague and misleading, so prompt the candidate to think about it.)*
Dates 'from and to'.
Where applicable, department or section in which employed.
Name and appointment of person to whom directly responsible. *(Required in any event for subsequent reference action — preferably by telephone — this question conveys a subtle hint to the candidate that, just perhaps, it would be better not to indulge in embroidery.)*

Kindly provide a *concise* statement of your main duties and responsibilities.

Kindly provide a *concise* indication of any personal limits of authority (relating to capital/revenue expenditure, etc.).

Where applicable, kindly provide *precise* details of the reasons for the termination of this employment. *(Note that, for those candidates still in post, we are not interested in finding out at this stage of the game why he/she wishes to change jobs — such comments as 'To improve my career prospects' are worthless. Probing of this type should be reserved for the interview — that is, if you really must do it at all.)*

Salary details. *(Or are you only posing this question in order to improve your chances of getting the candidate 'on the cheap'?)*

Details of any fringe benefits. *(To which the same comment applies!)*

And so on . . .

If you agree, and you jolly well should, that applicants' spare-time interests provide a good indication of any 'fire in the belly', then pave the way for an effective interview by posing the right question on the application form:

Kindly provide a *concise* description of your spare-time interests and leisure pursuits (with particular reference to your depth of involvement, attainments, etc.).

Some organisations like their application forms to have a crafty sting in the tail — and pose such beasties as *'Kindly provide a brief account of your medium- and long-term career objectives',* or *'Kindly state why you consider you are particularly suited to the post for which you are applying . . . '* These invitations to flannel are , of course, sixty-thousand-dollar questions and only serve one true purpose — an opportunity to assess the applicant's powers of written expression. Remember, there are no 'correct answers' to such questions, and any attempt by the short-lister to assess other than the ability of the candidate to string words together will be fraught with danger.

Lengthy 'health questionnaires' seem to be very much in fashion . . . You know the type of thing I mean — *'Indicate with a cross any of the following ailments from which you have suffered or for which you have received treatment during the last ten years . . . '.* I have seen lists of ailments that start with horribly terminal nasties, plough in descending order through a wide range of mental and physical ills — and end up with such pearls as back-ache, stomach troubles and the like. Who the hell hasn't had back-ache or tummy troubles? If the organisation is seriously interested in medical standards, why does it not pose the simple question, *'Are you willing to undergo a medical examination by the company doctor?* — and then apply the remedy?

'Maximum space'

Go on, be a devil — drag out a copy of your application form and inspect it in the cold light of day. Does it pose a question (or two, or three . . .) of considerable merit and importance, and then proceed to afford 2 x 5 cm of space for the candidate's minimum two-sentence response? The friendly reminder to resort to a separate sheet of paper when stuck for space hardly ever seems to work — so, if you really want maximum detail, for goodness sake give 'em the space in which to bare their souls.

Good luck — and good composing!

RECOMMENDED READING LIST

Anstey, E., *An Introduction to Selection Interviewing*, HMSO (1977).
Anstey, E., and Mercer, E.O., *Interviewing for the Selection of Staff*, George Allen & Unwin (for the Royal Institute of Public Administration) (1956).
Barrett, R.S., *Performance Rating*, Science Research Associates, Chicago (1966).
Bassett, G.A., *Practical Interviewing: A Handbook for Managers*, American Management Association, New York (1965).
Cronbach, L.J., *Essentials of Psychological Testing*, Harper & Row (1969).
Denerley, R.A., and Plumbley, P.R., *Recruitment and Selection in a Full-Employment Economy*, Institute of Personnel Management (1968).
Fletcher, C., *Facing the Interview*, Unwin Paperbacks (1981).*
Fraser, J.M., *Interview Case Studies*, Macdonald & Evans (1957).
Fraser, J.M., *Employment Interviewing*, Macdonald & Evans (1966).
Mandell, M.A., *The Employment Interview*, American Management Association, New York (1961).
Sidney, E., and Brown, E., *The Skills of Interviewing*, Tavistock (1961)

*Clive Fletcher's book is directed almost entirely at the *interviewee* — and is therefore 'required reading' for the astute *interviewer!*

INDEX

135

136